THE Transparent Leader

Dwight L. Johnson

HARVEST HOUSE PUBLISHERS
Eugene, Oregon 97402

Cover design by Koechel Peterson & Associates, Minneapolis, Minnesota

THE TRANSPARENT LEADER

Published by Harvest House Publishers
Eugene, Oregon 97402

The transparent leader / [edited by] Dwight Johnson with Dean Nelson.
p. cm.
ISBN 0-7369-0458-1(Trade)
ISBN 0-7369-0815-3 (Cloth)
1. Leadership—Religious aspects—Christianity. I. Johnson, Dwight, 1938- II. Nelson, Dean, 1954-

BV4597.53.L43 T73 2001
253—dc21 00-067307

Printed in the United States of America.

01 02 03 04 05 / BP-MS / 10 9 8 7 6 5 4 3 2 1

Contents

Foreword by Tim LaHaye 7

Dedication to Tom Landry 9

A Message from Tom Landry 11

1. True Power and Security
Chuck Colson 15

2. Following the *Real* Leader
Ken Blanchard 31

3. Finding God's Balance
Jerome A. Lewis 47

4. Living Out God's Vision
John Couch 57

5. Changing Your Course
Adolph Coors IV 73

6. Getting Past Superficiality
Vince D'Acchioli 89

7. Seeking God's Heart
Bill McCartney 109

8. The Character of the Leader
James H. Amos, Jr. 123

9. Mixing Faith with Business
Chuck Buck 133

10. Intimacy
Ronald Harris 143

11. Living Out Your Values
Dick Capen 157

12. Shaping the Second Half of Your Life
Bob Buford 169

13. The Role of Challenges in Our Lives
Hank Brown 181

14. Understanding Your Condition
Will Perkins 187

15. A Map, a Compass, and a Rudder
Sam Addoms 197

16. God Calls Us to Participate
William Armstrong 207

17. The Loneliness of Command
Bill Williams 229

18. Character Is More Important Than Success
Dennis Shaw 241

19. Living with an Eye on Eternity
Dr. William McColl 257

Acknowledgments

The Transparent Leader is the fulfillment of an idea that has taken many hands to bring to fruition.

I would like to thank Art Miley for suggesting that I write a book and Steve Deal for his encouragement and support. Also, thanks to Tim Philibosian for his support and participation. Doug Jackson introduced me to Dean Nelson, who has done a fine job in shaping the manuscript. Thanks also to Alma Harris for her work on the project. Rich Boyer introduced me to Bob Hawkins of Harvest House Publishers. Thanks to Bob and his great staff who were fabulous to work with.

A special appreciation goes to my family. First to Betsy, my love, my partner, my wife for 40 years. I love you. Also to our three sons:

—Dwight Jr. and his wife, Trish, and their three children, Shea, Emily, and Adam

—Eric and his wife, Jenny, and their children, Cooper and Cassie

—Stephen, a student at Point Loma Nazarene University, who graciously helped me with my computer needs

I'm also grateful to my mother, Edith Jane Johnson, and my late father, Ralph Johnson, and to my siblings, Ruthanne Jansen and Ed Johnson. The three of us were blessed to grow up in a fun-loving and happy Christian family.

Finally and most importantly, to our heavenly Father, God, who sent His Son, Jesus Christ, that we might have eternal life.

Foreword

We live in a culture that has twisted some very important words and concepts into tools of self-indulgence and self-promotion. In some cases, words and concepts that we should be embracing have become either meaningless or, worse, something to avoid altogether.

Words like *leadership* and *integrity* still have value today because they're often associated with power and authority. But what about words like *authentic, vulnerable, intimate,* and *transparent*? Are those words that are normally associated with leadership or success? Sadly, no. Instead, these words have become equated with one of the worst things you could call a leader today: *weak*.

The current business model would have us believe that a leader who is vulnerable or transparent before employees, customers, or stockholders will create a lack of confidence and put the business in peril. This book, *The Transparent Leader,* looks at it a different way. A better way. A way that was modeled after the teachings of the greatest Leader of all: Jesus Christ.

My friend Dwight Johnson has put together this collection of life stories from some of his friends who have excelled in business, politics, education, medicine, and public service. You may recognize some of their names as men who have changed how the world looks at a particular field. But I hope you'll recognize something beyond the names. I hope you see what I saw in this book. I hope you see a theme from each of these people that success often comes after profound failure or loneliness, after a dark night of the soul, after feeling abandoned by loved ones and by God.

Success becomes redefined when we bring ourselves before God and allow Him to transform us. Success means living a Christ-centered life, using the gifts God has given us to accomplish His goals in the world. This book shows how the world takes note of leaders like this.

I hope you'll see how each of these men became transparent before God, and then had the courage to let God use that transparency so that others could see God through them. It may seem like a new way of looking at leadership, but it's really quite an old concept, because this is how Jesus led.

The Transparent Leader is a book that should be on every business leader's desk and in every business school's library because it identifies an aspect of leadership that has been ignored for too long, and yet has been in evidence in the lives of many true leaders for centuries.

In leadership, pretense will only get you so far. Manipulation will only last so long. Control will endure only for a while. But being who you really are, being transparent, allowing the traits of Christ to shine through you, will lead you into eternity.

Now *that's* leadership!

—Tim LaHaye

Dedication to Tom Landry

When I first had the idea for a men's book on leadership, it was my friendship with former Dallas Cowboys coach Tom Landry that gave me the idea for the title, *The Transparent Leader*. To many observers, Tom seemed anything but transparent. A generation of football fans watched him each week as he stood stoically on the sidelines sporting that unmistakable fedora. But Tom was more than just one of the greatest football coaches of all time. He was also one of the great leaders of his generation. And to those who knew him, Tom was indeed a transparent leader. He openly shared his faith in Christ in word and deed, and amidst his many successes was quick to give other people the credit they deserved. There was nothing false or hidden about Tom Landry.

Tom's ability to influence others for good was especially brought home to me the year that Tom came to Denver to be the keynote speaker for our Colorado governor's prayer breakfast. At that time, my sons Eric and Dwight Jr. were six and nine years old and had attention spans of between two and three minutes. But that day they had raced home from school just to see the famous coach of America's favorite team: the Dallas Cowboys. That afternoon, Tom sat on the couch with one boy on each side of him for nearly an hour and shared with them why his quiet times with the Lord, both in the morning before he started his day and in the evening before he went to bed, were the most important parts of his day. Dwight Jr. and Eric are grown now, but so impressed were they that this famous man would emphasize this priority with them, that they have each maintained a regular quiet time ever since.

For six years Tom and I served together on the Fellowship of Christian Athletes national board of trustees, and during that time Tom and I got to know each other quite well.

When I shared the concept of *The Transparent Leader* with Tom and told him that he had inspired the title, Tom offered to write a foreword for the book. He not only knew a number of the men who had agreed to be in the book, but he also thought it was desperately needed.

Although he passed away before the book was completed, Tom finished the promised foreword. As a special tribute to a great man and to acknowledge his part in this project, I'm including verbatim Tom's foreword.

Thank you, Tom, for the friendship and for the incredibly positive influence you had in my life and in our family's spiritual growth.

A Message from Tom Landry

It's a charge I've heard my entire life: "Tom Landry? The man has no emotions! No feelings. No passion. Why, he never even smiles!"

Such statements don't bother me much anymore. Twenty-nine years as head coach of the Dallas Cowboys cured me of that. Also, no one who knows me well would voice those thoughts.

I'm passionate about many things, especially God, people, and football—in that order. That's one of the reasons I became involved with the Fellowship of Christian Athletes (FCA), a group that brings together three of my greatest interests: relationships ("Fellowship"), Jesus Christ ("Christian"), and sports ("Athletes").

My wife, Alicia, and I had heard about FCA in the early sixties. One summer, we decided to attend one of its conferences in Estes Park, Colorado. After going through the cafeteria line at our first dinner, we looked for a place to sit and spotted a couple of young men with some empty seats next to them. I introduced my wife and myself to those at the table and sat down. Little did I know at that time that FCA, Estes Park, and one of those young dinner companions, Dwight Johnson, would become a familiar part of my life for years to come.

In 1969, I was asked to join the FCA's national board of trustees. For the next several years I was able to observe Dwight's contributions in vision and management, as well as in finance, to FCA's outreach and impact. In 1972, we asked Dwight to join the national board, becoming the Rocky Mountain area's first board representative.

During that same year, Dwight asked me to speak at the Colorado governor's prayer breakfast, an opportunity I was pleased to accept. This event sticks in my mind because I feared I might have to cancel as a result of a recent foot surgery that necessitated my use of crutches. Dwight assured me this would be no problem. When he picked me up at the airport for the event, I discovered the reason he was so confident: He was also on crutches as the result of a skimobile accident. Quite an inspiring pair we were, struggling with luggage, a car, and crutches.

In 1978, John Erickson, then president of the FCA, approached me to say the board had decided to establish the Tom Landry & Associates membership in FCA. This would be done both to honor my participation in FCA and to encourage significant financial participating in its ministry. Those giving 10 thousand dollars or more per year and at least 100 thousand dollars over a lifetime would be made members of the Associates. It was not until years later that I found that the one who had conceived the idea, made the board motion, and written the first check, along with his wife, Betsy, was Dwight Johnson.

When God asks us to get involved with a venture, He charges us to do it with everything we have, with all of our heart, soul, mind, and strength. We are challenged to work energetically and wholeheartedly for the Lord. I have tried to honor those goals in my career in football.

Wanted: Men of Integrity

There is a desperate need for men who take such challenges seriously in business. Unfortunately, many men today do not even realize the enemy is engaging us in battle. The lines are drawn, but so many people fail to recognize the opposition's game plan. We need men who are observant, men who are committed and courageous, men who will not back down when the fighting is rough. We need men who understand biblical principles of leadership. The world is crying out for fearless heroes who evaluate the opponent's strategy, recognize the goal, focus on the objective, and commit to prevail. We need champions who know how to get others involved and keep them motivated until the end.

One such man is Dwight Johnson. He is unafraid to let the light of Christ shine through. He is willing to tell of his own weaknesses, his own struggles and fears. He is transparent.

As a result, God has worked frequently through Dwight to influence men in business, involving and inspiring them to share their lives, hearts, minds, and work opportunities with others so that they, in turn, may be motivated to excellence. This book relates the inspiring efforts of such focused men. As you read of the way they have allowed God to use them for His purposes, you will be challenged to be more transparent and vulnerable in your own life.

I never dreamed that God would use me in the way He did. All I had to do was follow His lead, and He took care of the rest. All I had to do was recognize and admit my own weaknesses, commit them to God, persevere in the truth, and be transparent with my own life.

As the lives of these vulnerable businessmen—men who are committed to following Jesus Christ—become known to you, I trust you will respond as I did: with a profound outpouring of gratitude for what the Lord is doing.

God is working through transparent men in the business world today. I find that exciting.

Why, it's so exciting that it almost makes me smile!

Many of us remember the Watergate scandal that resulted in the resignation of President Richard Nixon. One of the many names that Americans heard on the nightly news during that difficult period in America's history was that of presidential aide Charles Colson, often referred to as President Nixon's "hatchet man." For his role in the scandal, Chuck was sentenced to prison.

Later, Chuck admitted that although his sentence was one of the lowest points in his life, it ended up teaching him the greatest lesson he ever learned: He had to first lose his life as a power broker and hatchet-man attorney in order to find his life as a follower of Jesus Christ.

As a result of his experience, Chuck launched Prison Fellowship Ministries in 1976 following his release from prison. In 1979 representatives from Prison Fellowship groups sprang up around the world and formed Prison Fellowship International, which has more than 83 charter ministries and is the largest prison ministry in the world. In the United States, Prison Fellowship has more than 60,000 volunteers who reach more than 250,000 prisoners and their families each year.

Chuck continues to lead Prison Fellowship as chairman of the board. He and his wife, Patty, spend most of their time in Florida where Chuck continues to write monthly columns, editorials, speeches, and books.

1

True Power and Security

Chuck Colson

LIFE, I HAVE DISCOVERED, IS A SERIES OF paradoxes. Every few years this country celebrates yet another anniversary of Watergate. Where else but in the United States would you celebrate the anniversary of a burglary, and a bungled one at that? Typically, all of the network television crews come around and do interviews with me. Mike Wallace did a special two-hour program about Watergate at the twentieth anniversary. "Nightline" with Ted Koppel, the "Today" show, "Good Morning America," have all done anniversary stories on it, and I have been on them all.

Mike Wallace, at the end of a long, long interview asked, "Chuck, how do you now look back upon Watergate?"

I said, "Mike, I thank God for Watergate." He looked at me with a startled expression, and I continued. "Through Watergate I learned the greatest lessons of my life. The teaching of Jesus is true when He said, 'He who seeks to save his life will lose it. He who loses his life for my sake will find it.'"

I suspect that Mike Wallace is still sitting, scratching his head, saying, "All these years later, and that fellow Colson still speaks in riddles." Yet, I believe that if my life stands for anything, it's for the truth of what Jesus taught His disciples about finding our lives as we lose them for His sake.

I grew up during the Great Depression years. As a grandson of Swedish immigrants, I watched hungry people standing in bread lines and thought to myself, "The most important thing would be if I could ever go to college." No one in my family had gone to college. I had that great sense of wanting security and wanting to find my meaning, my purpose in life, wanting to get a good education and a good job. Then I won a scholarship to Brown University and graduated with honors. During the time of my graduation, America was fighting the Korean War, so I joined the United States Marine Corps and was commissioned a lieutenant. I remember the day I put the globe and the anchor of the Marines on my uniform, feeling great pride as an American in the United States Marine Corps tradition. I remember thinking, "This is my meaning. My security is as a Marine officer."

When the war ended I returned home, entered night school, and earned a law degree. I remember thinking, "I'll find my security, my meaning, and my purpose as an attorney." I started a law firm, and it grew and became very successful. I entered politics and became the youngest administrative assistant in the United States Senate. I remember thinking, "I'll find my meaning and purpose in law and politics."

The law firm continued growing and becoming more successful. I went up the ladder and, at age 39, was asked by the president of the United States to join him and serve as his special counsel.

The White House works just like many businesses. When I went to the White House I had an office way down the hall from President Nixon. Over time I moved closer and closer until I ended up in the office immediately next to the president of the United States. I remember one day looking out over the south lawn, over the beautiful, manicured, green grounds of the White House and thinking to myself, *My father was right when he told me during the Depression years, "If you work hard, if you put your mind to something, if you really go for it, you can succeed and achieve the American Dream."*

There I was, sitting in the office next to the president, walking in and out of his office every day of the week. It was one of the most powerful positions in the world. Limousines waited for me outside. Admirals and generals saluted me. It was everything a person could want. Curiously though, despite all of this success, I had the gnawing realization that I was as empty inside as ever.

After the 1972 election when President Nixon was reelected, I decided that having served in the government for four years was enough. I figured I was a little burned out. I had a beeper that went off at all times, a telephone beside my bed, the president calling at all hours, crises day and night. I decided that was why I felt so tired and empty inside. It was time to go back to my family and back to my law practice. And around this time, the Watergate scandal was just getting started.

Back to the Private Sector

One of the first things I did after leaving the White House was go back to Boston as general counsel to Raytheon, one of the largest corporations in America at the time. Its president, Tom Phillips, was a good friend of mine, but I hadn't seen him during my four years in Washington. I had always admired Tom. He had started out at the company at age 25, one of 50,000 employees. He went to engineering school at night and, at age 36, became executive vice president. Tom was a dynamic, hard-charging guy, and by age 40 he was president of Raytheon.

On this particular day, I walked into his office and I could tell right away that something was different about

Tom. Fifteen minutes into the conversation he began asking me about my health and how I was weathering what was becoming the great Watergate controversy.

After answering, I said, "Tom, something's different about you. What's happened?" He looked me square in the eye and said, "I have accepted Jesus Christ as my Savior and committed my life to Him." This caused me to take a firm grip on the bottom of my chair. I had never heard anyone talk that way. I thought only little old ladies in tennis shoes who stood on street corners handing out tracts talked like that. I mean, here is a seasoned, practical businessman—an engineer—talking about Jesus Christ as if He were here today! I had studied about Jesus when I went to Sunday school. I knew He was an ancient historical figure. But my friend was talking about Him as if he knew Jesus personally. I nervously changed the subject.

I then returned to Washington and was counsel to Raytheon and many other companies. Over the next months the Watergate scandal deepened. Patty and I would wake up in the morning and look out at our driveway to see it filled with camera crews. I was called before grand juries and investigating committees during this very ugly time in America. But all through this viciousness, every time I was with Tom Phillips from Raytheon, he still had that marked difference about him. He was kind, civil, decent, and seemed to care about me as a person. One night I went back to visit him in his home, and I asked, "Tom, you simply have to tell me what's happened to you. Why are you so different? What's this business about Jesus Christ?"

Tom's Story

Tom told me the most amazing story about how he, too, had started out with nothing in the world, how he had risen to a position of power, how he was the head of this huge corporation, had a beautiful home, wonderful kids who attended the best schools, had a Mercedes in the driveway. He had everything a person could want, yet he felt empty. He told me about going outside and looking at the stars and planets and galaxies all in perfect harmony and order, and as a scientist knew that there had to be something behind this perfect order. So he began a search for God. He read about Eastern religions. He read philosophy. Finally, one night while in New York on business, Tom read in the newspaper that Billy Graham was preaching that night at Madison Square Garden. He had never heard Billy Graham, but he went to the arena, got a seat in the upper stands, and heard a sermon on who Jesus Christ really is. Billy Graham preached that Jesus isn't just an ancient historical figure, but the Son of the living God who rose from the dead and who lives today and who knocks on the doors of our lives and asks to come in. My friend Tom Phillips, head of one of the largest companies in America, sitting in the upper stands that night in Madison Square Garden, made his way down through the crowd, stood before the stage, and gave his life to Christ.

Afterward, everything about his life began to change. The hole inside began to fill up. His relationship with his family deepened. His attitude toward his business changed. As he told me this wonderful, moving story of his conversion, he read to me from an incredible book called *Mere Christianity,* written by Oxford scholar C. S. Lewis, one of the great intellectual giants of the twentieth century. Tom read the chapter called "The Great Vice," which says pride is something we see in everyone else and never in ourselves. A proud man always walks through life looking down on other people and things, Lewis said. But when you're looking down, you don't see anything above yourself. You don't see God. C. S. Lewis didn't know it when he wrote those words back in the 1940s, but he was writing them for Chuck Colson.

My Decision for Christ

As I listened to my friend that night, I realized that pride had driven me all those years. I thought I was looking for security, power, and influence because I wanted to take care of my family and because I was idealistic about service in government. In reality, I was driven by my own pride.

Tom wanted to pray with me that night, but I didn't do it. I was too proud. I was a friend of the president and a big-time lawyer in Washington D.C. He wanted me to pray, sitting right there in his living room. I had never done anything like that. I had prayed by rote in church, but nothing like what he was suggesting. I said, "No thank you." But as I left Tom's home that evening, I borrowed his copy of *Mere Christianity.*

I bid Tom a good night and walked out to my car. At that time I had the reputation of being the toughest of the Nixon guys, the White House hatchet man, the ex-Marine captain. But that evening as I slid into the driver's seat, I found that I couldn't get the keys into the ignition. I was crying too hard. I sat for a long time in my friend's driveway thinking about my life, thinking about what he had told me about Jesus, and wanting more than anything else in the world to know God and be at peace with Him. Finally, sitting there alone in my car, utterly aware of my own powerlessness, I cried out something like, "Take me, God. Take me the way I am!"

The next morning I was sure that when I woke up I would feel embarrassed at what I had done. But I didn't. Instead, I felt a wonderful, wonderful sense of peace.

My Faith on Trial

Shortly after that I went to Washington D.C. and someone noticed me attending a prayer breakfast at the White House. If you knew anything of my reputation at the time, you would understand the reaction of the Washington press corps when they discovered that Chuck Colson, of all people, was attending a prayer breakfast. There was hilarity in the press room at the White House, with reporters patting one another on the back, throwing newspapers in the air. I kept the cartoonists of the United States fed and clothed for a full month, and the cartoons were all essentially the same: Chuck Colson kneeling in front of the White House with a big sign that said, "Repent." Some cartoons had President Nixon looking outside, saying, "Help! Call Billy Graham! Colson's got religion!" Stories about my conversion went all over the world, and it was the frequent subject of network television coverage.

During the next few months I realized that my newfound Christian faith was more on trial than anything I had done in Watergate. So one day I walked into the prosecutors' offices and told them that I couldn't plead guilty to what they were charging me with, but I *was* guilty of other things. I told them of something I *had* done and said that if they wanted to charge me, I would plead guilty. I can tell you that, if you're ever in a similar circumstance, prosecutors are amazingly obliging under those circumstances. As a result of my plea, I received a one- to three-year sentence.

Interestingly, it was in prison that I learned the two greatest lessons of my life. I had been in politics. I had been in government, sitting at the right hand of the president of the United States, because I had been idealistic and wanted to change government. I wanted the power to be able to bring my own conservative political convictions to government. The amazing thing is, as I look back on those four years, practically nothing changed.

Every day the limousine would drive me to the office. I would have a big stack of briefing papers piled up in the backseat, and as I was driven through the gates of the White House, the guards would salute. I would go up to the second floor of the West Wing of the White House where the 12 senior aides of the president of the United States would gather every morning at 8:00. This routine would happen every single day. Henry Kissinger would be the last one to come in. He would have a worried, dour look on his face, big briefing books under his arms, and he would begin the meeting the same way every day. Foreign policy was always at the top of the agenda. "Mr. President," Kissinger would say, "the decision we're going to make today is going to change the whole future course of human history." Every day, five days a week, 52 weeks of the year, it would be like that. And as I looked back, I realized that we didn't change much. Maybe we made some changes in how we dealt with the news media or how we dealt with Congress, but not with how people really lived.

With Christ in Prison

It was in prison that I discovered the source of real power for change. The terrible thing about prison wasn't so much the physical deprivation. I had been in the Marines. I could live in just about anything and get used to it. But I could never get used to seeing men lying on their bunks and staring into the emptiness with nothing to do, no place to go, nobody caring about them, their bodies atrophying, their souls corroding.

Seven of us formed a prayer group. Three were black, four were white: two dope dealers, a car thief, a stock swindler, the former special counsel to the president of the United States, and two others, on our knees at night, praying and studying our Bibles together. Other prisoners would come by and we would talk to them. They asked what we were doing and we told them what it meant to repent, to really know Jesus Christ, to turn their lives around, to be transformed. We would see these men give their lives to Christ and the next day their very stride was different—they walked without the prison shuffle. Their heads were up; they were transformed by the power of the living God.

People think the White House is where the power is. It's not. I saw in prison, where people were powerless, that the only power that really mattered was the kind that changes a human heart. And that can only happen through Jesus Christ, the Son of the living God.

The other important lesson I learned was that all I had invested in striving to get to the top, to achieve success, power, money, fame—I found it all meaningless. In prison, with all of those things gone, I found that the only identity, security, and meaning a person ever has is when he or she is at peace with God and knows Him personally. When you have a personal relationship with God, you know who you are and why you're here and where you're going. All my years of looking for security—my education, my job, my military appointment, my position in government—ended up with my finding true security in God.

I identify with Alexander Solzhenitsyn, one of my heroes, who spent years in a Soviet gulag. From the gulag he wrote the most memorable words written in the twentieth century. He said, "Bless you, prison. Bless you for being in my life. For there, lying on the rotting prison straw, I came to realize that the object of life is not prosperity as we are made to believe, but the maturing of the soul." The maturing of the soul is the object of life. That is why I could easily say to Mike Wallace, "Yes, thank God for Watergate."

With that look to my past, I want to also look to our future as a nation. It's important for leaders in this culture to see how they can proclaim the gospel in all that they do, and to understand why it's important that they do so. It's important to understand the future we're all trying to affect. Just as it was important for me to discover where true power is, I think it's necessary to see that power applied to our workplaces.

I believe that there's a struggle occurring today in regard to our future in general and our culture in particular. I think each of us has an obligation to recognize deceptions in the culture that are incompatible with our faith and to expose them. Those deceptions may very well be at work in the organizations where we are employed.

The Myths of the Four Horsemen

There are four great myths of our times, which I call the four horsemen of the present apocalypse. The first myth is that of the goodness of man. The first horseman rails against heaven with a presumptuous question: "Why do bad things happen to good people?" He multiplies evil by denying its existence. This myth deludes people into thinking that they're always victims and never villains, always deprived and never depraved. It dismisses responsibility as a teaching of a darker age. It can excuse any crime, any bad behavior, because it can always blame something else, like a sickness of society or a sickness of the mind. One writer calls it "the golden age of exoneration." But when guilt is dismissed as the illusion of narrow minds, then no one is finally accountable. The irony is that this should come about in this century with its gulags, death camps, and killing fields. As companies and as individuals we must not diminish the importance of being accountable for our actions.

G. K. Chesterton said that the doctrine of original sin is the only philosophy empirically validated by centuries of recorded history. Many people remember the story of Yehiel Dinur, the Holocaust survivor who was a witness at the trial of Adolph Eichmann. Dinur stared at the man who had presided over the slaughter of millions and began to sob. He collapsed, not out of bitterness or shock at seeing the butcher, but from the terrifying realization that he, the survivor, was capable of doing what Eichmann had done. Eichmann is in all of us.

The second myth of modern culture is the promise of the coming utopia. The second horseman arrives with sword and slaughter. This is the myth that human nature can be perfected by government. This myth says the New Jerusalem can be built using the tools of politics. Ruthless ideologies have moved swiftly from nation to nation on the strength of a promised utopia. They pledged to move the world but could only stain it with blood. We saw more people killed last century by their own governments than in all of its wars combined. We have seen every utopian experiment fall exhausted from the pace of its own brutality. Yet, utopian temptations persist, even in the world's democracies. The political illusion still deceives, whether it's called the Great Society, the New Covenant, or the New World Order. Each one promises government solutions to security, peace, and meaning, which can only really be found in the human heart. As leaders, we must put our faith in God, not in systems that continue to fail in delivering on their promises.

The third myth is the relativity of moral values. The third horseman sows chaos and confusion. This myth obscures the dividing line between good and evil, noble and base. It has created the great crisis of our day—a crisis in the realm of truth.

When a society abandons its transcendent values, each individual's moral vision becomes purely personal. Society then becomes merely the sum total of individual preferences, and since none is morally preferable, anything that can be dared is permitted.

This leaves the moral conscience for our laws in tatters. Moral neutrality slips into moral relativism. Tolerance substitutes for truth, indifference for religious conviction. In the end, confusion undercuts all of our creeds. It is possible for organizations to stand for something. It is possible for leaders of those organizations to articulate the values they stand for that transcend the groups they are leading.

The fourth modern myth is radical individualism. The fourth horseman brings excess and isolation. This myth dismisses the importance of family, church, and community. It denies the value of sacrifice and elevates individual rights and pleasures as the ultimate social value. But with no other principles to live by, men and women suffocate under their own expanding pleasures. Consumerism becomes empty, leaving society full of possessions but drained of ideals. This is what Vaclav Havel calls "totalitarian consumerism."

A psychologist tells the story of a young, despairing woman who is exhausted from an endless round of parties in the pursuit of pleasure. When she went to the psychologist for help he said, "Why don't you just stop what you're doing?" She looked at him and said, "You mean I don't have to do what I want to do?" As author George MacDonald once wrote, "The one principle of hell is, I am my own." Leaders of this country need to live responsible lives of principle and conviction, pursuing truth, not greed.

I have seen firsthand the kind of society these deadly myths create. I have visited more prisons than I can count, in more nations than I can name. I have seen the crisis of modern times in human faces. They aren't just in prisons. They are in our companies, our political groups, and our churches. Many of our coworkers wear those faces.

The Hope of the Cross

As the world looks to us, let us summon the courage to challenge our comfortable assumptions, to scrutinize the effect we're having on our neighbors, and then recover that which has been the very soul and conscience of civilization.

It's easy to become discouraged, but the Christian has neither the reason nor the right, for history's cadence is called with a confident voice. The God of Abraham, Isaac, and Jacob reigns. His plan and purpose rob the future of its fears. By the cross He offers hope. By the resurrection He assures triumph. Mankind's choice is to recognize God now or in ultimate judgment. Do we welcome His rule in our lives or fear it?

In the aftermath of the tragedy in Waco, Texas, and terrorist bombings in New York, we heard dire warnings about religious extremists. But I don't think they are the world's greatest threat. Far more dangerous is the decline of true religion and of its humanizing values in our everyday lives. True faith in God shows itself in humility. It shows itself in peace. It shows itself in service. It builds communities of character and compassion. On occasion, God gives us glimpses of His glory. I witnessed one in an unlikely place—a prison in Brazil—a glimpse like none I have ever seen.

Several years ago this Brazilian prison was turned over to two Christian laymen. Their plan was to run it on Christian principles. The prison has only two full-time staff. The rest of the work is done by inmates. Every prisoner is assigned another inmate to whom he is accountable. In addition, every prisoner is assigned a volunteer family from the outside who works with him during his term and after his release from prison. Every prisoner joins the chapel program or else takes a course in character development.

When I visited the prison I found the inmates smiling—particularly the murderer who held the keys and opened the gates to let me in. Wherever I walked, I saw men at peace. I saw clean living areas. I saw people working industriously. The walls were decorated with biblical sayings from Psalms and Proverbs. The prison has an astonishing record. The recidivism rate is four percent, compared to 75 percent in the rest of Brazil and the United States. How is that possible? I saw it with my own eyes. When my inmate guide escorted me to the notorious punishment cell once used for torture, he told me that today it houses only a single inmate. We walked down a long cell block, a long corridor of steel doors, and came to the end, and he peeked in. He paused. "Yes, he's in there," he said. Then he turned to me and asked, "Are you sure you want to go in, Mr. Colson?"

"Of course," I replied impatiently. "I've been in punishment cells in 600 prisons all over the world." Slowly the inmate swung open the door, and I saw the prisoner in the punishment cell. I walked in and turned to the right and, there on the wall, beautifully carved by the inmates, was a crucifix. The prisoner Jesus was hanging on the cross. "He," said the inmate, "is doing the time for all the rest of us." In that cross, carved by loving hands, is a holy subversion. It heralds change more radical than mankind's most fevered dreams. Its followers expand its boundaries of a kingdom that can never fail, a shining kingdom that reaches into the darkest corners of every community, into the darkest corners of every mind. It's a kingdom of restless virtue and endless peace. The work proceeds, the hope remains, and the fire will not be quenched.

We all see the culture we are a part of, and yet we don't have to be overwhelmed by it or ruled by it. Once we truly see the activity of God in society and in our lives, we are free to create His world in our workplaces and homes. It is our task. It is our privilege!

We serve a God who saves, who turns power upside down, who conducts heart surgery, who stands in the prison for us. Employees, customers, clients, and family members will see Him through us. As people see Christ in us, as their hearts change the way mine did, the myths and fears of the culture are destroyed, and the future is secure.

It was about ten years ago that I first met Ken Blanchard at an executive outreach breakfast. The group was small, so we were able to have some fairly intimate discussions among ourselves. When it came time for Ken to share, he told us about his spiritual journey. He was named after a Presbyterian minister and attended church regularly as a youngster. But gradually he drifted from the church. In the late 1960s he turned his back on religion completely when a minister friend of his was fired in the most unchristian way by his congregation for leading sit-ins and protests over the Vietnam war and other social issues. He and his wife Margie decided "if that's what Christianity is all about, they can have it."

It wasn't until the incredible success of his bestselling book *The One Minute Manager*, coauthored with Spencer Johnson, that he began to undergo a spiritual renewal. Over time the Lord became central in his life. Today many of his activities are focused around The Center for *FaithWalk* Leadership, which he cofounded with long-time colleague and friend Phil Hodges. His chapter "Following the *Real* Leader" is an outgrowth of this work.

The One Minute Manager has sold more than nine million copies worldwide and has been translated into more than 25 languages. This classic still appears on bestseller lists almost 20 years after its first publication. Ken's other bestselling books include *The Power of Ethical Management*, coauthored with legendary positive-thinking minister Norman Vincent Peale, and *Leadership by the Book*, coauthored with Bill Hybels, founding senior pastor of Willow Creek Community Church, and Phil Hodges.

Ken is chief spiritual officer of The Ken Blanchard Companies, which he founded in 1979 with his wife, Margie. The organization's focus is to unleash the power and potential of people and organizations around the world for the common good.

2

Following the *Real* Leader

Ken Blanchard

I AM A FOLLOWER OF JESUS. REGARDLESS OF your faith or your place in life, whether you're a parent, a business manager, a schoolteacher, or a volunteer, I am convinced that Jesus is a leadership model for all leaders.

Look at what He did. He hired 12 incompetent people who didn't have any of the skills relevant to the job ahead. He could have at least picked some decent preachers. The only one of the 12 who had any education was Judas, and he turned out to be His only turnover problem. For a long time I've said, "The important thing about being a leader is not what happens when you're there, but what happens when you're not there." It's easy to get people to do what you want them to do when you are hovering over them. The key to your effectiveness is how well your followers carry on when you're not around. Did Jesus' leadership create anything that lasted? You'd better believe it. Here we are 2000 years later, still talking about His influence.

The first time I ever thought about Jesus as a leadership role model was shortly after *The One Minute Manager* was published in 1982. It became so popular so quickly that I was asked to appear on Robert Schuller's "Hour of Power" at the Crystal Cathedral. Reverend Schuller asked me, "Do you know who was the greatest One Minute Manager of all time? Jesus!"

"Really?" I said.

"Sure," he answered, "Think about it. Jesus practiced the three secrets of the One Minute Manager—One Minute Goal Setting, One Minute Praisings, and One Minute Reprimands. After His goals were clear as to why He had come, He managed by wandering around from one little town to the next, catching people doing things right and then praising or healing them. If they got off base, He wasn't afraid to redirect or reprimand people. He was a classic One Minute Manager."

This was the beginning of my examination of my own faith because the more I became exposed to followers of Jesus, the more I realized that everything that I had ever taught or written about, Jesus did. The minute I became open to a spiritual awakening, all kinds of people started showing up in my life to help my journey.

On God's Team

One of the first spiritual people to come into my life was Norman Vincent Peale, the positive-thinking pastor. He was 86 when I first met him and still very active. I'll never forget what Norman said to me at one of our first meetings: "Blanchard, the Lord has always had you on His team—you just haven't suited up yet." That statement stuck with me until several years later when I first met Bill Hybels, senior pastor of the legendary Willow Creek Community Church in South Barrington, Illinois, and asked him, "So, how do I suit up?"

"It's easy for a One Minute Manager," Hybels answered. "Whenever you're ready, just put your head down and say, 'Lord, I can't save myself. I fall short of perfection. I accept Jesus as my savior and bridge between me and You.'"

Of course I resisted suiting up for a while because as Norman Vincent Peale had told me, "The toughest test of self-esteem is to bow your head and turn your life over to the Lord. The human ego doesn't want to give up that kind of control." Given that reality, it wasn't until about nine months later when we were having a major problem with our company that I "bit the bullet."

A business executive we had made president was causing a lot of trouble. As I was driving to meet my wife, Margie, to talk about what we should do, I suddenly realized, "Blanchard, you are so stupid. Why are you trying to figure this all out by yourself?"

Hybels had told me, "The great thing about Christianity is that you get three consultants for the price of one. You should understand that, Blanchard—you're a consultant. You get the Lord, who created it all. You get the Son, who lived it, and you get the Holy Spirit, who is your day-to-day operations manager. Why don't you take advantage of their expertise?"

So as I drove up the interstate, I simply prayed and turned my life over to the Lord. It became clear to me that I couldn't figure this or anything else out by myself. I needed His help. And as I prayed, I could feel a peace come over me. My life has never been the same. One time after I had taken the Lord into my life, I asked Dr. Peale, "Should I stop what I'm doing and go back to divinity school?"

He was quick to answer, "Absolutely not. You have a tremendous congregation out there, and we just don't have enough preachers in the field." As a result, my personal mission became to be a loving teacher and example of simple truths that help myself and others awaken the presence of God in our lives. My commitment and the commitment of The Center for *FaithWalk* Leadership is to help leaders walk their faith in the marketplace. To me, that means teaching them how to be the servant leader that Jesus wants them to be.

Learning to Be a Servant

In Matthew 20 Jesus took the disciples away to tell them that He was going to be arrested, falsely convicted, and crucified. Right after that John and James began to argue about who should sit on Jesus' right or left side in heaven. They were vying for power. When the disciples heard them arguing, they became angry. Why? Probably because they wished they had thought of that first.

After spending three years with Jesus, you would have thought they all would have known better. If I were Jesus, I would have fired them all. But what did Jesus do? He saw this as a teaching opportunity. He had incredible patience. He said:

> You know that the rulers of the Gentiles lord it over them, and their high officials exercise authority over them. Not so with you. Instead, whoever wants to become great among you must be your servant, and whoever wants to be first must be your slave—just as the Son of Man did not come to be served, but to serve, and to give his life as a ransom for many (Matthew 20:25-28).

That doesn't sound to me as though Jesus was offering a plan B. He wanted his disciples to be clear that if they wanted to be first, they had to be last. If they wanted to lead, they needed to follow. He who is the humblest is the greatest.

As a result of Jesus' mandate, I am asking people, "Are you a servant leader or a self-serving leader?" When I first started asking that question, I was a little arrogant—as if to say, "I've got it, baby, and you don't." Finally I realized that we *all* tend to be self-serving leaders to some degree. After all, our original equipment heart is self-serving.

There's nothing more self-serving than a baby. I never heard of a baby coming home from the hospital saying, "How can I help around the house?" We all let our egos get in the way. To my way of thinking, "ego" stands for "edging God out" and putting self in the center of the universe. As a result, our journey from a self-serving heart to a servant heart is a never-ending one.

Why? Because we all fall short of perfection.

Scoring 100

I remember that when I was seriously examining my own faith, one of the things that bugged me about Christianity was the concept of original sin. Why do we have to start off bad? It didn't make any sense to me. I'm a humanist—why not believe in original potentiality?

Then I ran into Bob Buford, the author of that fabulous book *Halftime*.

"Bob, why this original sin stuff?" I asked him.

"Blanchard, do you think you're as good as God?" he asked.

"No, of course not. If there is a God, that's perfection." I answered.

"Okay," he said. "Let's give God a 100 and ax murderers a 5. We'll give Mother Teresa a 95—she was a pretty good person. You're not bad, Blanchard, because you're trying to help people, so let's give you a 75."

I was able to follow him this far.

"The great thing about Christianity," he continued, "is that the Lord sent Jesus down to make up the difference between you and 100."

That made sense to me. I could more easily accept that I'd fallen short of 100 than someone calling me a sinner.

"Before you get too excited though," said Buford, "let me tell you something you might not like as much. The ax murderer has the same shot at the ball as Mother Teresa. Grace is a gift; it depends on your acceptance of Jesus as your savior, not your performance."

I remember when I first found out that Peter Drucker, the great management guru, was a believer. I asked him why he was a Christian.

He answered, "There is no better deal. Who else has the gift of grace?"

Hybels told me that the difference between religion and Christianity was in the spelling. Religion is spelled D-O. To get grace, there is a "to do" list of things you have to do to measure up. Christianity, on the other hand, is spelled, D-O-N-E. The Lord sent Jesus down to take care of our sins because we all fall short of 100.

Remembering Our Priorities

So what's the journey in life? It's to enjoy a relationship with the Lord that operates every single day out of love rather than false pride. Every morning our ego is there trying to lure us afresh into believing that gaining earthly success is what life is all about; that the meaning of life is found in trying to meet our ego's insatiable hunger for praise and acceptance from others. It's a constant battle.

Some days turn out better than others, but the secret is to remember our priorities. Tom Landry knew that secret. Some days the Dallas Cowboys won; other days they lost. Someone once asked him how he remained so calm during a game that's as incredibly competitive as professional football.

"It's easy," he answered. "My priorities are in order. First comes my Lord, second comes my wife, third come my kids, and fourth comes my job. So if I lose on Sunday, I've got a lot left over."

When businessmen are controlled by their ego, their identity is determined by whether they win or lose. They become their accomplishments—or their defeats. Self-serving leaders, led by their egos, care about gaining and maintaining power, status, and position.

If you give them necessary negative feedback, they kill the messenger. Why? Because they have to protect who they are, and who they are is their position. If they lose the ball game on Sunday, they've got nothing left over.

Servant leaders, on the other hand, are really there to serve. If a better leader comes along, they're willing to step aside, willing to partner. They love feedback—even negative feedback—because it tells them how they can be better.

Sometimes when I mention this concept of servant leadership, people say, "I don't want to be a servant leader because it's all about pleasing everyone. It's all about being liked."

Did Jesus please everyone? Was He liked by everyone? No. He was in the faces of all kinds of people. Who did He really want to please? His Father. His Father had a vision and a mission. That's what Jesus came to do—to live out and communicate the vision and the mission of His Father.

The vision part of leadership asks, "Where are we going?" A lot of organizations don't know where they're supposed to be going or what business they're really in. But it's important to know where you're going because leadership is about leading somebody somewhere. Even Alice in Wonderland learned that truth. When she got to a fork in the road, she asked the Cheshire Cat, "Which road should I take?"

"Where are you going?" he asked.

"I don't know," she answered.

He said, "Then it doesn't matter which road you take."

Likewise, if you don't know where you're going, your leadership doesn't matter.

Values and a Clear Vision

At our company, the mission is "to unleash the power and potential of people and organizations for the common good." Our motto is "we're the world's number one advocate for human worth in organizations." Our three ranked values are first, *ethics*—doing the right thing; second, *relationships*—building mutual trust and respect with our customers, suppliers, employees, and the community; and third, *success*—running a profitable, well-run organization.

Every morning I deliver a brief devotional to our company via voice mail. I remind everyone (we have 250 people working with us) of where we're going and why we're doing what we're doing. I'll never forget asking one CEO what his job was as head of his great company. He said, "I play the visionary role, and I have to be like a third-grade teacher in communicating it. I say it over and over and over until people get it right, right, right!"

A clear vision starts it all, and concentrated focus on that vision determines whether people are going to be energized. All great organizations have someone at the top saying, "This is where we're going, this is what we stand for, this is what we believe in."

If you talk to anyone at Ritz Carlton, whether they're an hourly front line associate or a senior vice president, and ask what the mission of Ritz Carlton is, they'll tell you: "To be the number one hospitality provider in the world." Their motto is: "We are ladies and gentlemen serving ladies and gentlemen."

Until vision is clarified, servant leadership behavior can't kick in. Because what are you serving if you don't know where you're going?

In addition to vision, there's another important element in this kind of leadership. It's called implementation. It addresses how you get where you want to go.

"Quack, Quack, Quack"

You can always tell organizations that are run by self-serving leaders because implementation to them means protecting the hierarchy. People in these organizations actually think that some people are superior and others are subordinate. Their department heads have hired hands. The hands don't get to have heads! When people say, "I'm in supervision," they somehow think they see things better. What they really have is a duck pond. What do ducks do? They go, "Quack, quack, quack."

You can always tell an organization that's in trouble and that has self-serving leaders. When a problem exists, front-line people will say, "Quack, quack, it's our policy. Quack, quack, I just work here. Quack, quack, I didn't make the rules. Quack, quack, would you like to talk to my supervisor? Quack, quack, quack."

Everybody is serving the hierarchy.

This was vividly illustrated to me several years ago when my wife and I flew into Sydney, Australia, at about 8:30 A.M. on a holiday weekend. The hotel where we were staying didn't allow check-in until 3:00 P.M., so we stopped by to drop off our bags so we could walk around Sydney. As we arrived, a fabulous woman greeted us and gave us a letter from the general manager who told us how important we were. "I'll keep your bags here until we get a room for you," the lady said.

"Great," we said.

"Is there anything else I can do for you?" she asked.

"Yes," I said. "I need to cash a traveler's check."

"Oh, no, I can't do that!—quack, quack!" she answered.

"Why not?" I asked.

"I don't have your room number—quack, quack!" she said.

"But you have our bags," I replied.

The situation just unraveled immediately over a systems issue. This poor woman suddenly started to quack. "Quack, quack, look, I just work here; don't give me a hard time." It was evident that management had told their people, "You follow the rules. Leave your brains at home. Pick them up after work, because they aren't going to be any good around here."

Turning the Pyramid Upside Down

Years ago I got to write a book with Don Shula, the legendary coach of the Miami Dolphins. He said that he became a great coach when he realized that he couldn't throw a pass, couldn't make a kick, couldn't make a tackle.

As a result, he felt his job was to help his players to do those things well. Therefore, in a sense, Shula felt he worked for them.

Don was always the first one on the field, and the last to leave. He did whatever it took to prepare and help his players to be the best. Where did he get his strength and support? Shula said, "My day started best when I was on my knees thanking God and asking for help."

For servant leaders, the normal pyramid of how things work has to be turned upside down. How many of you have gone to your boss's house, and the first thing he did was take off your shoes and socks and wash your feet? And yet that's what Jesus did for his "employees."

Why? Because it was one last chance for Him to demonstrate to His disciples what they needed to know about servant leadership. Later they would have ministries that thrust them into leadership roles. Now, before His departure, He was telling them, "Go out and share the good news that I have brought you. Go out and serve the mission. Go out and serve what we are trying to do."

When I was a college professor, I got in trouble because on the first day of class I handed out the final examination. The rest of the faculty asked, "What are you doing?"

"We're supposed to help the students, aren't we?" I asked.

"Of course," they replied. "But you're not supposed to give them the questions for the final."

I answered, "Not only am I going to give them the questions, but during the semester ahead, I'm going to teach them the answers so that when they take the final exam, they'll get A's. Life is all about getting A's, not about some normal distribution curve."

That didn't sit too well with my academic colleagues.

Remember, the Lord didn't use the normal distribution curve with us either.

We're in Sales, Not Management

Once I asked Norman Vincent Peale if he believed that Jesus is the way, the truth, and the life.

"Absolutely," he answered.

"So what about the millions of people who never heard of Him?" I asked. "And what about the millions of good people who heard about Him and decided not to follow Him?"

"I believe in a loving God," he said. "I'll bet He handles that in a loving way. I'm in sales, not management."

As Christians, we're all in sales. We're recruiting for the kingdom of God. And our mission isn't necessarily about results. It's more about what we can do to help. What can we do to support? What can we do to get people on the program?

That's opposed to the natural lure of earthly success, which is usually about money, recognition, and power. That's what most people push and shove for. Nothing is bad about any of those things, in and of themselves. What's bad is when you judge who you are by them. If you have a fair amount of money, is that really an indicator of great success? No, because those who look to their bank account for success find that they soon have to go out and get more money, because what else are you going to do for your next act? If you've got some recognition, you had better go get recognized more. If you have power, you had better get more. These earthly appetites are never satisfied. The cry is always for more.

The opposite of these earthly pursuits is spiritual significance. Instead of money, the issue is generosity. The Lord doesn't mind if you have a bunch of money, but He loves to see what you do with it. What's the opposite of recognition and achievement? Service. What's the opposite of power and status? Loving relationships.

It All Goes Back in the Box

John Ortberg, one of the wonderful pastors at Willow Creek Community Church, tells a story that puts this all in perspective. When he was young, John's grandmother was an incredible Monopoly player. He said that whenever she came for a visit, the two of them played Monopoly. Grandma was absolutely vicious at the game. At the end, John said he always had nothing and Grandma had everything. Then she would smile and say, "John, someday you're going to learn how to play this game."

One summer a kid moved in next door who was also a fabulous Monopoly player. So John practiced with him every day because he knew his grandmother was coming to visit in September. When she arrived, John gave her a big hug and kiss and said, "Grandma, how about a Monopoly game?" Her eyes lit up and she said, "Sure, John." But he was ready for her this time. He wiped her out. He destroyed her. He had everything. At the end of the game his grandmother smiled and said, "John, now that you know how to play the game, I want to teach you a lesson about life. It all goes back in the box."

"What do you mean?" he asked. "This is the greatest day of my life! I want to have the game bronzed!"

She said, "No, it all goes back in the box. Everything you bought, everything you accumulated."

Think about that incident in relation to your life. If your ego is in the way, and you're pushing and shoving as a self-serving leader for wealth, recognition, power, and status, the sad thing is that when life ends, it all goes back in the box. The only thing you get to keep is your soul, and that's where you store who you loved and who loved you.

Run, Shaya, Run

I heard a story recently that helps put it all in perspective. It was about a little boy in New York named Shaya. He was a special needs kid. Intellectually and physically he couldn't keep up with the other kids his age. Sometimes his father would get upset about it and say, "If the Lord is about perfection, and He's the Creator, where is Shaya's perfection? Why is he the way he is?"

One day he found out.

He took Shaya to the park, and there was a group of the neighborhood kids playing baseball. As they headed across the park, Shaya asked his dad, "Do you think they'd let me play?" His dad's heart sank because nobody would ever choose Shaya. He was fearful, but when he looked at his face and his excitement about possibly playing, he went over to one of the kids on the sideline waiting to bat and said, "Could Shaya play with you?"

The boy looked at him with a blank look, then went over to his teammates and asked, "Can Shaya play?"

One of the kids said, "It's the bottom of the eighth, and we're six runs down. Why not?" So when they made their third out and went into the field, they put Shaya right behind the second baseman in the shallow outfield so he couldn't do too much damage. Miraculously, for the first time in the game, their opponents got three straight outs, and the neighborhood boys were up to bat again.

Suddenly the team came alive. They started scoring runs. Then the bases were loaded, and the winning run was at the plate, and it was Shaya's turn at bat. His father thought, *They'll never let Shaya bat because he can't hit*. But this was a day of amazing events, and the kids let Shaya bat. When he got to the plate, the opposing pitcher moved as close as he could to throw a gentle pitch Shaya's way. He took a swing and missed wildly. His father thought, *Oh no, he's going to strike out. They're going to lose, and Shaya will be a failure again*. But one of the kids on Shaya's team got up and went behind him, put his arms around him, and held the bat with Shaya. His father thought, *I know the other team will stop this. They won't allow that.*

But nobody said a word. The pitcher moved to the front of the mound and threw the same gentle pitch toward Shaya, where now there were really two people batting. They hit it, but it was just a dribbler to the pitcher. The father thought, *Oh no, it's an easy play. Throw to first, the game's over. The team loses. Shaya fails again*.

The pitcher fielded the ball and threw it with a high arc over the first baseman's head. Shaya's teammates yelled, "Run, Shaya, run!" He ran to first, and then headed to second. The right fielder had the ball by now, and the father thought, *Oh no, an easy throw to second, and Shaya is out, and they lose. He fails again*. But the right fielder not only threw the ball over the second baseman's head, but over the third baseman's head, too, into the stands. The team yelled, "Run, Shaya, run!"

As he approached third base, all 18 kids began yelling, "Run, Shaya, run," including the kid holding the ball. When Shaya got across home plate, both teams picked him up and carried him around the field. And the father thought, *Now I see Shaya's perfection. It's in causing others to reach out in love.*

We all fall short of 100. We're all Shayas at one point or another. If we can be people, organizations, cities that help the Shayas God sends our way, it helps us all, because our egos are out of the way.*

If we do it right, we aren't going to have to put one bit of it back in the box.

* The story of Shaya is from the book *Echoes of the Maggid* by Rabbi Paysach Krohn, published by Mesorah Publications.

I first met Jerry and Martha Dell Lewis shortly after Jerry started his Petro-Lewis Corporation, which became one of the largest oil and natural gas partnership companies in the world.

There was a tremendous amount of energy business activity around Colorado in the 1970s and early 1980s. President Carter named Denver the energy capital of the world, and that action sent Jerry and the other energy leaders into orbit. Petro-Lewis took off on a growth curve that was practically straight up. The public stock made the Lewises multimillionaires overnight.

Jerry worked very hard to handle all of this sudden success. He was involved with several accountability groups, and they helped him through the days when very volatile oil prices created unusually large peak and valley swings in the industry. Jerry saw a need for men to be able to fellowship together and come alongside one another when a member of the group was having a difficult time. Some of the groups he organized have been meeting for 40 years.

With all of the business and spiritual opportunities they had, they always made their three children the priority. As a result, a lot of the activities at the Cherry Hills and Vail homes were family-oriented and in association with the ministry of Young Life. Jerry served on their national board for more than nine years and helped to shape the lives of hundreds of young people.

When the bubble finally burst on the oil industry, the Petro-Lewis stock started downhill from a high of 42 dollars a share. Jerry saw what was happening, but by the time he was able to reduce his operation enough, it was too late to save the company. As a result, he started looking for options and was finally able to sell the company for 73 cents a share and at least give the creditors and shareholders something for their money.

Jerry lives with his wife, Martha Dell, in Denver.

3

Finding God's Balance

Jerome A. Lewis

DURING MY EARLY YEARS AS A BUSINESSMAN, my understanding of God was that He was someone who sat up in heaven with a great big balance scale. I knew that in my life the sin side was loaded down very heavily, and I hoped and prayed that before I died I could get the scales back in balance.

Through the years I had heard a lot of preaching and learned a lot of swear words about Jesus, but He never was part of the formula necessary for my life. Concepts such as forgiveness and salvation through grace were completely foreign to me. All I knew of Christianity consisted of the legalistic dos and don'ts I had learned as a child.

My wife was the same way. She taught Sunday school in church back in those days and often says, "I wonder what I was teaching those poor kids!" I must have had a similar teacher in my childhood. My spiritual health was just above baseline—a little higher than indifference. I had what I considered a socially acceptable spiritual life, a proper one.

I grew up in Wichita, Kansas, having the advantage of a wonderful, loving, and prosperous extended family. I had many friends, adequate intelligence and education, some recognition and athletic ability, and a sound moral upbringing. My wife and I met at the University of Oklahoma, and after graduation I worked for the Shell Oil Company, and then in the family business. We belonged to a fine country club, and my wife was in the Junior League. We were going along at a fairly even keel.

"Eat, Drink, and Be Clever"

Then, at age 41, my life changed so dramatically that it has never been the same. I had started a little company called Petro-Lewis, and when I went public with the stock, the price soared from 5 dollars per share to 20 dollars in six months. I had made so much money by the time I was 42 that I was ready to wheel and deal. My operational philosophy became "eat, drink, and be clever." I partied and traveled and flirted every chance I got. I was able to develop an impressive image of success and sophistication, discussing who I knew and where I had been. I was pretty good at it, too.

But as my business success and net worth increased, my spiritual health decreased. It was almost a mirror image, working in an inverse proportion. The better off I was materially, the worse off I was spiritually.

Since childhood I had heard biblical teaching from my grandmothers and from church and Sunday school. In high school and college I went to church occasionally. As my wife and I were raising our kids, we hopped from one church to the next, trying to experience something that had meaning. All we knew about church was that we were supposed to go and supposed to give it some money occasionally.

None of that really mattered during my increasing success, even though I drank more, needed more pills to help recover in the morning, and needed wilder companions to accompany me on wilder trips. I went from New York to Los Angeles to Vegas constantly. Those were heady days.

The truth is, I would really like to forget those days. All of our kids were in big trouble. We searched for something meaningful for them—and unconsciously, I'm sure, for ourselves. Fortunately, we found a group of truly different people in the staff of Young Life, a Christian youth organization. They were attractive young adults who were fun to be around and who acted differently from most teenagers. They also weren't afraid to talk openly about Jesus Christ. Our kids got somewhat involved as we pushed them into it, but my wife and I got very involved. Right after Petro-Lewis went public, I magnanimously agreed to help Young Life cover the deficit they had at the end of their fiscal year. I began to meet with them once a week, presumably to give them financial advice for the coming year so that the deficit wouldn't happen again. But before we could talk finance, they would make me sit and wait for them to talk about the Bible, talk about kids, talk about their lives. After hanging around like that for a year, I began to understand something about Jesus. But I didn't let it foul up my life. I was able to continue my decadent lifestyle.

We used the money we made on our stock increase to merge companies with a cattle-feeding operation owned by my brother-in-law. That was a mistake. A year later the deal exploded. When we got into the cattle business we had one million dollars in equity in Petro-Lewis. Eighteen months later we had lost two and a half million dollars. Our cash position was in crisis, and our banks, investors, and employees panicked. So did I.

This was during the days before cell phones, so I dodged the office and the phones by driving around in my car all day. I had all the typical behavior of someone who was trapped. I didn't want to talk to anyone. I had no family life. I hardly knew my kids—they avoided me and I avoided them. In fact, I avoided everyone—except for the four guys from Young Life.

A Prayer of Surrender

It all came to a head one December morning. I'll never forget driving downtown to work to face another hopeless meeting with my managers. On my way there I realized I no longer had any answers, and for the first time in my life I was ready to give up. And that's what I did. I was all alone in the car, stopped at a red light, and I just shouted, "Okay, God, You run my life. I give up. I'll put this whole mess in Your hands, if You want it."

What felt like a 300-pound gorilla leaped off my shoulders. Tears of joy welled up to where I couldn't see, and people behind me started honking because the light had turned green—literally and spiritually. All I could do was laugh and motion for them to go around me. The hardest thing in life for me—probably for anyone—is to give up control, but now it had happened. And I was free.

I wish I could say that things immediately got better, but they didn't. They got worse. The bankers quit, our directors quit, people sued. My brother-in-law sued me for ruining his cattle business, and the stock in our company dropped out of sight. But I knew that a miracle had occurred. There was no hope left, but somehow I was smiling now, and no one could understand why.

Back on Top

One Los Angeles banker retained his belief in us, and he helped us save the company. Then things really took off. The oil business was good then, and when oil prices went up we jumped on the bandwagon. Eventually we became the nation's largest sponsor of public oil and gas programs. In one 12-month period we raised 803 million dollars, and over nine years we raised 3 ½ billion dollars. We were the nation's second-largest independent producer of U.S. oil and gas. We were also one of the nation's largest users of bank credit. We had a bank line of 1.6 billion dollars with 17 banks around the world. We were also the first oil business to use junk bonds. We were the third largest employer in Denver and rented more than one million square feet of office space. Two of the largest financial transactions in the country at the time involved us, when we bought properties from the Hunts and from Dupont. We had 2200 employees in 17 states. Our oil and gas reserves had grown from about one million barrels, worth about 1 dollar per barrel, to 400 million barrels worth 10 dollars per barrel. Our assets grew from about 1 million dollars to 4 billion dollars. Our stock split 13 times, which made us the darlings of Wall Street.

While the company was growing financially, I was growing spiritually. My hopelessness was gone, obviously because the price of oil had gone up. But the things I was known for, like my catchy phrases, arrogance, greed, envy, vengefulness, and autocratic nature, seemed to soften and diminish because my brothers in Christ kept pecking away at me. They seemed to know every time I had a lustful thought, or when I got too engrossed in my press clippings or self-importance.

It was great fun for my wife and I to rebuild our marriage, to mend our relationship with our kids, and to celebrate the grandkids who started arriving. It was a joy to run a large company, to offer employment to the Young Life people, to encourage our employees to get involved in ministry and civic activities, and to give away money. We gave away huge amounts, and it was fun. We were personally experiencing the Lord's blessings, living our faith rather than reading about it. Still, I wasn't very spiritually mature.

At our zenith, when I was 55, I had the opportunity to sell half of my stock for more than 30 million dollars and set up a substantial charitable organization, which I had always wanted to do. However, as unbelievable and egotistical as it sounds, I felt I could make more by not selling. The investment was still in my name, and I felt that even though it was the Lord's investment, and I had dedicated it to the foundation, the stock had a lot more potential because it was undervalued. What a joke. Naturally, everyone thinks his stock is undervalued. I have never met anyone who thought it was *overvalued*. I just felt that I could do a lot better with this asset, which would provide me a larger tax deduction. You can guess what happened during the next four years as the price of oil dropped. Our stock price per share went from 42 dollars to 73 cents.

When the price started down, we found antagonists everywhere. They included bankers, investors, brokerage firms, class-action attorneys, the FCC, the IRS, shareholders, landowners, bank examiners, and the press. One day I picked up the Wall Street Journal, and on the front page the feature article on the right-hand column was about me. It was complete with my portrait, mustache and all. That was the crowning blow of the press coverage, because every day there had been an article in the Denver paper. But now it was national. My friends stayed away from me in droves. Fortunately, there were a few who stood by me. My wife, thankfully, remained my partner. And my Christian fellowship group of six or eight guys was just a phone call away.

Avoiding Bankruptcy

The next two years felt like a lifetime. We did everything imaginable to survive. We sold 25 percent of the oil and gas assets for one billion dollars so we could pay off almost all of our bank debt. That got the bankers off our backs. Then we raised hundreds of millions of dollars of debt and equity at expensive rates and terms. We settled a huge class-action suit, spinning off a royalty trust to investors. We went from 2200 employees to fewer than 400. We ate every bit of that leased office space, square foot by square foot. But the price of oil kept dropping, and we couldn't handle it.

To avoid bankruptcy we searched furiously for a merger, a partner, a buyer, in hopes that we could eventually benefit from a time when prices would go back up. This was the most stressful period of my life, because during the negotiation for a merger there were ugly proxy battles going on in the newspapers and all along Wall Street, with a lot of bluffing and bitterness between bond owners and us. Petro-Lewis managers were publicly castigated. But we were finally able to avoid Chapter 11 and the loss of our financial rights, with a little money to spare.

During those years the Lord gave me the ability to release to Him all the problems I had, which included the stark fear of losing all material assets. When business went bad 16 years before, I didn't have many assets, so losing them wasn't that great a shock. But this time was different, and yet I was still able to be resigned and somewhat peaceful about the possibility of losing everything. That experience gave me as big a boost in my spiritual life as when I came to Christ initially. I found out personally that the promises in Scripture are true.

The Lord really does answer prayers and guide our lives if we'll yield and surrender to Him. He really will raise us up on wings like eagles and give us wisdom if we need it. He really will give us peace that passes all understanding and power that exceedingly and abundantly works through us. He really will perfect His strength in our weakness and remold our minds from within, and actually will give us His mind. These are fantastic promises from God, and they're all true. In addition to His promises, God gave me the continuous love and encouragement of my wife. I would have never made it without her.

My 30-Million Dollar Lesson

Although I learned a lot going through this experience, it sure felt good when the testing ended and the merger finally closed. I learned something else during that time. It was a 30-million dollar lesson. Since I decided to not sell my stock because I thought I could do better, I ended up with a 98 percent decline. I think the Lord finally got impatient with my procrastination and my pride and my arrogance, and decided to give the money to someone else. I haven't found out who that was yet!

He still blessed me with the two percent left, which was substantial and adequate, so I deserve no sympathy. But I lost a great opportunity. One of the lessons people should get from my experience is that they should have some fun giving their money away now instead of waiting to multiply their wealth, or waiting to get a larger tax deduction, or waiting until after they die. We should be like Andrew Carnegie, whose strategy was to give away all of his money while he was alive, and to give it away boldly. One of the greatest freedoms we have in Christ concerns money. It's a difficult subject, but I doubt that any of us can understand the true freedom Christ talked about until we cease being slaves to mammon.

I had a 20-year roller-coaster ride in my material life. I had two highs, each higher than the last one, and two lows, each lower than the last. You could look at my life and call me a loser from Denver who ran his company into the ground twice. But through all that, I am more peaceful and joyful than I have ever been in my life. As an engineer, I've looked back on this time and plotted a graph of my life's ups and downs. The more detail the graph contained, the clearer the story became. Two graphs emerged. The graph of my material life went one way, and the graph of my spiritual life went the other. I would recommend that everyone consider doing this—graphing the oscillations in life. It's very revealing.

What Really Matters

After reaching a deplorably dead point at age 43, I came alive in Christ in a big boost upward. My spiritual life had a steady climb for 16 years, and as my material life plunged, it experienced another boost upward. The result was that I learned what it really meant to trust God. In the ensuing years, I have had continuing and deepening spiritual growth. If I look at the graph now, I feel that my spiritual life is on a geometric scale going upward, while my financial picture is stable. I have a deep desire to be with Christ more than to do things. I enjoy spending time in contemplation, solitude, and prayer. I read more and try to keep mentally alert and involved in business and social activities. I work out more, both physically and spiritually. I estimate that 25 percent of my time is with people, particularly with Christian fellowship groups. I can't stress how important it is to be a part of a fellowship of other believers with whom you can be open and transparent, especially during the hard times. Another 25 percent of my time is spent reading, studying, being with my family, and playing. But the other 50 percent is spent at the office. I still work on oil and investment deals, but also on ministry matters.

The peace in my life today is the result of finding a balance between being and doing, between business and ministry, between playing and working. God, in His grace, sustained me materially and spiritually, even though I did my best to destroy myself in both these areas. I had to experience His grace the hard way, much like the guy who had a serious heart attack. He was asked if he enjoyed his heart attack. He said no—it scared him nearly to death. Would he like to do it again? No. Would he recommend it? Definitely not. Does his life mean more now than before? Well, yes. Are he and his wife closer than ever? Yes. Does he have a new compassion for people, a deeper understanding of their predicaments? Yes. Does he know the Lord in a richer, deeper fellowship than he ever thought possible? Yes.

If someone asked you or me today how we liked our business failures and would we recommend them, how do you think we would answer? What *should* we answer?

John Couch has always been a man whom I have admired and respected since I first met him back in the late 1980s when he and his family moved to Rancho Santa Fe, California.

John had been one of the first employees Steve Jobs hired to work at Apple Computer after he noticed John's success with product development at Hewlett-Packard. Many people give John the credit for taking Apple from a start-up company to a firm doing one billion dollars in sales in its first five years of operation. By today's standards, one billion dollars in sales after five years is no big deal, but 20 years ago it was huge. John's success landed him in *Business Week, Fortune, Newsweek,* etc., and with an invitation to be keynote speaker for more than 2000 people at the Boston Computer Society.

In spite of his achievements, what impressed me about John was his transparency amidst his success. He said, "I wasn't even sure who I was, and it was very apparent that my wife and our four children were very sure that they didn't know who I was. That got my attention." The material success didn't make any difference to John's family. They wanted a father and a husband.

John and his wife, Diana, made the decision to sell their houses, step back from the "stuff accumulation" position with Apple, and concentrate on their family. He accepted the headmaster position with a struggling Christian school in Rancho Santa Fe and helped it become the successful school that it is today.

John and Diana have since moved back to Silicon Valley to be available for how God is next going to use him and his many talents.

4

Living Out God's Vision

John Couch

WHEN I WORKED AT APPLE COMPUTER IN 1978, we had a banner in the office that said, "The reward is in the journey." It meant that the destination—the results—weren't as important as what we experienced along the way. The results would come, but as a by-product of enjoying the journey. The important things were the friendships we made and challenges we met as we worked together to accomplish things that most people said couldn't be done.

I believe the truth of that banner, and as I think of my own journey, I can think of three distinct phases where there were rewards along the way.

The first phase was early in my life, when I was aware that there was a God. I grew up in a Roman Catholic family. We had a Bible, but it was a gold-edged, very colorful, gorgeous book that sat on the coffee table. It was never opened and never read.

The second phase was when I came to the Lord and started to study and live by the principles in the Bible.

The third phase was when I experienced the power of God's Word in my life.

Each of these three phases has an explanation.

When I was six years old, my father died at the age of 27. This tragedy forced my mother to go to work and, in a sense, I went to work, too. I became very independent and self-sufficient through my paper routes and everything else I could do. After high school I went to the University of California at Berkeley at a time when it was the only school in the country that offered a computer science degree.

There were no textbooks and very few professors. Most of the teachers were 20- to 22-year-old students fresh out of MIT and other engineering schools. As a result, we got to pave our own way through the educational process.

After college I spent six years working at Hewlett-Packard. During those years I was very driven in my pursuit of success. I managed 40 to 50 people, taught graduate school, and wrote a textbook at the same time. Spiritually I was in limbo. I knew *about* God, but didn't have a relationship with Him. He was someone I knew of, but at the same time, didn't know. Fortunately, I had a wife who was praying that the saving grace that she had found would come to me also.

The Apple Experience

One day Steve Jobs came to my home. It was a Friday, and he laid an Apple II computer on the kitchen table. He told my three-year-old son, Kristopher, "You can keep this if your dad comes to work for me."

What I saw that weekend was truly remarkable. For the first time I was introduced to possibilities I had never seen associated with computers. You see, when I left Berkeley in 1972, my home cost 25,000 dollars and the computer that I worked on cost a quarter of a million dollars. Only six years later we were looking at homes that cost a quarter of a million dollars and computers that cost 2500 dollars. There was a historic shift taking place in society, right before my eyes. We called it a paradigm shift, from the mainframe or time-shared computer that the business world knew to the desktop with its many possibilities for personal home use. At that time most people's concept of the computer was from George Orwell's book *1984* where computers were used to control people's freedoms.

That weekend I saw my son go places on that computer that he had never been before. I knew things were happening with him when the television didn't come on all weekend. On Sunday night I said, "Kris, don't get too attached to this device because I may have to return it."

"Why is that, Dad?" he asked.

"Well, if I don't take the job, it has to go back."

"Just say yes, Dad," was Kristopher's simple reply.

Well, I did say yes, and it changed my life, because in the next five years Apple went from seven million dollars to one billion dollars in sales and became the fastest growing company in the history of America at that time.

When I joined Apple, I probably raised the average employee age of Apple by several years. The company was very, very small at the time, and the first two software programmers I met were in high school. They had walked in the front door at Apple and said, "Look what we did with your Apple II," and Steve Jobs said, "You're hired." Steve was only 20 at the time.

It was quite a culture shock for me coming out of Hewlett-Packard for six years, where I had managed by walking around, and going to Apple where I was managing by running around!

I became even more driven than before. I enjoyed the celebrity status of being vice president of Apple Computer and all of the benefits that came with it—the stock options, the profiles in magazines. It was a remarkable time.

But although everything seemed wonderful, I was out of control and I didn't even know it. I was like the fellow who jumped from the 20-story building and, as he went by each floor, people inside could hear him say, "So far so good!" That was my life. I thought everything was great. The money was plentiful, the kids could go to whatever schools they wanted to, and my wife was a tremendous support to me.

Tug of War

God still played only a minor role in my life at that time. He was only a consultant to whom I went when things got too stressful. I was like the fellow who was late for a business meeting downtown and couldn't find a parking space, so he tossed up a quick prayer and said, "Lord, help me find a parking place." Just as he finished his prayer somebody pulled out and he said, "Never mind, God, I found one myself." I didn't have any peace in my life. Instead, I had a lot of stress, a lot of pressure, and I felt a constant demand to perform.

As you know, in the technology business whatever you do this month is obsolete six months later. You can be on the highest crest of a wave and a few months later you're out. I watched around me as people failed left and right. Some were smarter and had more experience than I did, and yet they were failing. I didn't understand what was propelling me forward within this intense environment.

And I *really* didn't understand the impact that it was having on my family.

Because I lost my father when I was young, I didn't want my kids to ever feel the loss I had felt. But I came to the realization that I didn't have to be dead to be missing in action. My travels and my 16-hour days, six days a week, were resulting in my kids not having a father. My daughter wrote a poem to me when she was 11 and called it "Tug of War." This is the wisdom of an 11-year-old girl:

I will not play tug of war,
I'd rather play hug of war,
Where everyone hugs instead of tugs,
Where everyone kisses and everyone grins,
And everyone cuddles and everyone wins.

In her wisdom she saw the tug of war that was taking place in my life. I was in the world, trying to be all those things I was brought up to live by, as stated in the Ten Commandments. I was trying to be a father, trying to be a husband, trying to be ethical, trying to be good, but it was *me* that was doing all the trying, and my kids could see the struggle inside me. I started to realize that the building I was living in was built on the wrong foundation. And God began sending me some clues to wake me up.

A good friend of mine, a Harvard undergraduate and a Stanford MBA, had started a company called Software Publishing. Then while skiing, he suffered a stroke at age 33.

I also started to see changes in the people around me at Apple. When Steve Jobs recruited me, it was with the concept that everything he had was through someone else's contribution to society. The car he drove, the home he lived in, the food he ate, the clothes he wore, were all the result of other people's expertise. What he wanted to do was take this technology and give it back to the individual. I admired that idea. But over time I saw Apple change. The people there started to believe all of the press hype written about them. I could see that the Lord was giving me a mirror into the future, because I wasn't very much unlike the others at Apple. So I knew I had to make a change. I had to build in some stoplights in my life.

The Decision to Resign

Finally I decided to resign. It was something no one at Apple understood. They simply said, "He's just burned out. Let's give him a year's sabbatical with pay and full benefits, and stick this resignation in the bottom drawer."

But that wasn't the answer I was looking for. I knew I had to make some drastic changes in my life. I did something that, I discovered later, could have put me in jail. I exercised my stock options and sold them the same day as a way of saying, "You know the resignation that was dated 90 days ago? You have to accept it now."

I didn't realize it at the time, but when I sold my shares in Apple, it was too late for the sale to occur that day. The next morning, the stock opened up 35 percent lower, which netted me 35 percent less than I expected. But it was all part of God's wisdom. If the sale had transpired that afternoon, without a doubt the SEC would have said, "You knew something, so you sold your stock as a company officer, and look what happened the next day." So even though I lost money, I felt that God was protecting me and honoring my decision.

At about the same time, I started attending a church, and the humility of the pastor there broke me. I had never met a man who was so humble and so at peace. Where I had been working, my life was surrounded by driven people. In the process of going to church and being under the ministry of this pastor, I turned my life over to the Lord and started to study His Word. That's when I read in James 1:17, "Every good and perfect gift is from above." All the experiences and everything that I had been given really had been given to me by God. I was extremely blessed.

But I was still searching. I knew that the path I had been on was leading me to destruction, and that I was empty. I kept asking God, "What is it that You have for my life?"

This was a difficult transition because that tug of war inside me was still taking place. There were two worlds at war. There was the world that I knew—living according to the dictates of society—and then there was God's way, which was new to me. This was the start of the second phase of my life: starting to know God by studying His Word.

I was challenged because James 1:22 also says, "Do not merely listen to the word, and so deceive yourselves. Do what it says." That's a very simple verse, but very, very difficult to live by. As I struggled with how to live that verse, I was faced with an unexpected temptation.

Lucas Films called. They were looking for a CEO. It was a tempting situation. My wife was excited because it would get me out of the house again. When you retire at the age of 36, it puts a lot of pressure on the family. I went from managing 300 people to managing five.

My kids were enthusiastic about the job offer and told me, "Gee, Dad, we would get free Star Wars toys! Take the job!" The temptation was to jump right back in the corporate world, but I knew that from a management standpoint, the challenge of working with George Lucas was not going to be any less than working with Steve Jobs. It would have been a very creative, exciting environment, but I didn't feel that it was what the Lord was calling me to do.

Instead, I felt that I needed to transfer the faith that I had been placing in things, friends, and my own personal comfort into faith in God. Someone once told me that when life is easy, possessions grow. But when life gets difficult, people grow. That was certainly true of the transition I was in. Things were easy at Apple. Sure, it was intense, but it was exciting. There was no distinction between life and work—you just gave everything.

If my wife had come to me and said, "John, you have to make a decision between your family or this vice presidency of Apple Computer," it scares me today to think of what decision I would have made. I was that caught up in the work.

"Let's Move!"

I continued to pray for God's purpose in my life. During that time I met a man who took me to a small school near San Diego called Santa Fe Christian School. I attended a parents' meeting, where there was a cry for help to keep the school open. Two things happened right after that. The first was that my daughter came home from the Christian school she attended in the Silicon Valley and said her school was a fake. "I can't get anybody to even pray for a basketball game," she said.

The second thing was that the Lord impressed my wife with Genesis 12:1,2, which says, "The LORD had said to Abram, 'Leave your country, your people and your father's household and go to the land I will show you...and I will bless you.'" All of a sudden my whole family said, "Let's move! Let's get out of this valley, let's get out of the temptations, let's get out of this environment." Within four days my wife, daughter, and cat were in San Diego, and I was in northern California with a very large house. My boys and I packed the U-Haul truck and headed south. The house and the furniture sat up north, unsold for three years, and I kept asking, "Lord, is this really what You wanted?"

At Santa Fe Christian School there was a wonderful spirit, so we enrolled our kids and I was asked to join the board.

This was during a time when most Christian television and radio programs were saying, "Gee, here's the vice president of Apple, and he turned his life over to the Lord. Let's get him in here to share his testimony." During that year I spoke to 70 or 80 different groups all over the country. But I realized that my heart was hard. I was playing the same kind of game with my new Christian brothers and sisters that I had played at Apple. At my old job I could stand in front of 2000 people, show off some new technology, and get standing ovations. I was seeing too many similarities between how I was at Apple and how I was giving my testimony. I had become a Christian cheerleader.

So I turned down all of my speaking invitations and continued to pray, "Lord, what is Your purpose for my life?" In response, God gave me the parable of the Good Samaritan. Where I had been thinking of working with Pat Robertson of the 700 Club, or James Dobson of Focus on the Family, and things of that level, God was asking me to meet the present need.

The present need. For instance, this local school called Santa Fe Christian. Now there was a present need. But I had no intention of going from Apple Computer to this small school. What would my friends Bill Gates and Steve Jobs think? But that was the present need that I saw, and God was asking me to meet it.

So I agreed to join the board, but more out of a responsibility as a parent because, as Proverbs 22:6 says, "Train a child in the way he should go, and when he is old he will not turn from it." I knew that being a responsible parent didn't mean delegating parenthood to the state or even to a Christian school.

The first board meeting was a disaster. It went from 7 P.M. to 2 A.M. and there were no objectives and a lot of infighting. The people's hearts were right, but they had no vision. I came home and said to my wife, "I think I made a mistake."

I thought that there would be peace and unity within a Christian organization. Then I went to the next meeting and found the same thing. By the third meeting I asked, "What vision has God given you for this ministry?"

No one could answer that, so I offered to write a business plan for them. I said that I would go to the school, talk to the teachers, the community, the parents, the students, and others, and that in three months I would have a plan.

What I soon discovered as I went into my data-entry mode was that the school was 300,000 dollars in debt, that it hadn't paid the agreed-upon rent, that it was losing 30,000 dollars a month, and that they had a 30-day lease on a property that had been sold to a developer who was going to turn it into condominiums.

Sitting in a room by myself with this realization, my first reaction was to say, "I'm out of here." The truth was that I was afraid to fail. Failure was never something the Lord had dished out to me. And I was very afraid of it. But the Lord convicted me like I have never been convicted before and drove me to my knees. It was as if He said, "What kind of Christian are you? I have given you everything. I gave you your wife, your youth, a beautiful family, a life-changing experience at Apple Computer, and now for the first time in your life that you can't see the light at the end of the tunnel, you want to bail out. *Where is your faith?*"

It was at that point that I understood what Abraham's test in Genesis 22 was all about. I had never understood why a good God would ask a father to sacrifice his own son. But in that moment it became crystal clear to me. The Lord was asking Abraham, "Do you love what I gave you more than you love Me?" And that was exactly what the Lord was asking me in this situation. I also felt a sense of freedom as I realized that the results were going to be God's responsibility.

If the school closed or stayed open, that was the Lord's doing. All He was calling me to do was to obey and serve. I realized then that, up until this time, I had been exchanging God's truth for a lie by worshiping and serving created things. In ancient Rome the people worshiped the creations rather than the Creator, and that's what I had been doing. I knew that bondage had to be broken. Zechariah 4:6 says, " 'Not by might nor by power, but by my Spirit,' says the LORD Almighty." It was at this point that I realized I had to enter the third phase of my journey, which was to experience God's power. I had to die to myself and let the Lord be responsible for the results.

The Shoulders of Giants

Sir Isaac Newton was once asked how he made so many discoveries. He replied by saying that if he has seen farther than other people, it was by standing on the shoulders of giants. I reflected on who the giants were in my life. Certainly, my newfound faith and relationship in Jesus Christ showed me that the answer was in His Word. I could stand on His Word and on the shoulders of the giants in the Bible. But I also reflected on what had made Apple such a success. Why did Apple succeed when other companies failed?

It occurred to me that Apple succeeded because they had a vision. Their vision was that the personal computer was nothing more than a mental bicycle. Just as God gave us talents to build tools to amplify our physical ability, He gave us the talent to build tools that would amplify our mental ability as well. This was more than taking us someplace where we had already been, more than running Cobal and Fortran on a cheaper computer.

This was about taking us places we've never been. That vision of the mental bicycle clarified Apple's purpose, which was one person/one computer, during a time when most of society thought of computer terminals as appliances tied to large computers in large corporations. That kind of innovative thinking was another good shoulder to stand on.

I prayed for vision, because in my studies I realized that vision comes from God. In the Old Testament, time and time again, Abraham, Joshua, Moses, and others received clarity to their purpose directly from God. So as I prayed for the future of Santa Fe Christian, God gave me the verse Ephesians 3:20: "Now to him who is able to do immeasurably more than all we ask or imagine..."

The verse told me that we have the power of the Holy Spirit to do things so much more abundantly than we perceive. It told me that God's vision was not to build a school for my kids, or even the neatest kids, but for all of God's kids. This was the vision for the school. That vision then clarified our purpose, which was to develop Christian leaders of tomorrow. And with that we wrote a plan.

The plan talked about spiritual growth, academic growth, social growth, and physical growth—consistent with Luke 10:27, which tells us that the greatest commandment is "'Love the Lord your God with all your heart and with all your soul and with all your strength and with all your mind'; and, 'love your neighbor as yourself.'"

Our plan addressed what it means to be a Christian, to be biblically based, to have a biblical worldview. We also addressed how we would use technology, and we said that we wanted to be able to master technology, not be mastered by it.

At Apple I had a saying: "I believe in miracles. I just don't believe in scheduling them." With this five-year plan for the school, I said to God, "Okay, Lord, You're in the miracle business. You schedule it, we'll serve."

A Plan in Three Phases

The plan was very simple. Phase I was to communicate the vision to the teachers and parents so they could take ownership. It was a way to stake a flag that said, "The Lord has given us a vision in Ephesians 3:20 that's way beyond anything any of us can comprehend, but it's His ministry and, if we serve, we will be on a journey that will be very exciting."

In response to our plan, God started with the miracles. First, the city of Solana Beach voted to incorporate, and suddenly all building permits were frozen, so the condominium project on the property where we were was put on hold. Then the Lord simply provided for us. One Friday we weren't able to meet payroll, and I prayed very earnestly about it that evening. The next morning I got a call from a lady who wrote a check to Santa Fe Christian School that exactly matched the payroll.

During this time, a lot of healing took place among some of the groups that had formed in opposition to one another.

In the first five years, the school grew from 220 students to 600, and I was named headmaster.

The second phase of our journey came during the time that I personally was experiencing the power of God's Word. We were able to purchase the property at the school, and then we grew to more than 800 students. Somehow, someway, the Lord brought more than 6.6 million dollars into the school without any formal organization. It took nine years before the tuition covered the cost of operation. If I had run an operation like this in Silicon Valley, I would have been fired five times over. But it's not how we planned it—it's how God did it.

In Phase I God had told us to get our community to share the vision. Phase II was to implement the vision, so we built a technology base that would allow us to put our curriculum into a digital platform.

Phase III was to make the curriculum available to the world. I didn't know how all of this was going to take place ten years ago. But today, we have fiber optics in every classroom and the ability to share the curriculum over the Internet. We can use the Internet to tell truths, and we must do so.

The Internet is definitely being used by Satan as a snare. If you think television captured the hearts and minds of our children, wait until you see the junk that's out there on the Internet. Yet at the same time, as Christians, we want to establish truth on the Internet.

The challenges we faced at the school were amazing, unbelievable. We were at capacity for our students and said, "Lord, we haven't even met the needs of Your community, much less Your kids—where do we go from here?" We were at a critical phase as to what direction we should go.

But our focus was on Christ. We were challenged to not focus on the financial aspect, but to communicate that God had brought us through this time and that He would take us forward whether or not the numbers showed it. Which, of course, He did.

As I look back on this journey and the rewards I've experienced along the way, I think of the promise God has given in Jesus' Sermon on the Mount: "Blessed are the pure in heart, for they will see God."

Our heart's condition is much, much more important than our work position. That's a lot of what the journey is really about—a conditioning of our hearts. When our hearts are right, God will give us a vision that will clarify the purpose of life. Then we will become not great men of God, but men of a great God.

I first met Adolph Coors IV when my wife, Betsy, joined a women's organization called the Junior League. Husbands were often invited to events sponsored by the group, and it was at one of these functions that I was introduced to Ad Coors.

As a young man Ad idolized his father, and was devastated when his father was suddenly taken from him. The events surrounding that loss have had a profound impact on the man that Adolph Coors has become, as you'll read in the following pages.

Many of us think how nice it would be to be born into the right family with the right last name. Ad is a living example that having the courage of his convictions and pursuing the plan that God has for his life have been more important than an earthly heritage.

Ad has spent the past 20 years of his life traveling around the country telling his story of how God's grace not only saved his life, but also his marriage and his calling as a man of God. Ad and his wife, B.J., have two grown sons and three grandchildren and make their home in Colorado.

5

Changing Your Course

Adolph Coors IV

ONE FOGGY NIGHT, THE CAPTAIN OF A LARGE ship saw what appeared to be another ship's lights approaching in the distance. The two were on a course that would lead to a certain head-on collision at sea. Quickly the captain signaled, "Please change your course ten degrees west." The reply came blinking back through thickening fog: "You change your course ten degrees east."

The captain, now insulted, decided to pull rank, as he angrily sent a message back. "I am a sea captain with 35 years of experience. Change your course ten degrees west!"

Without hesitation, the signal flashed back, "I'm a seaman, fourth class. You change your course ten degrees east!"

The captain became enraged. Realizing that they were rapidly approaching one another and would most certainly collide in a few moments, he sent his final warning. "I am a 50,000-ton freighter. Change your course ten degrees west *now!*"

A simple message came blinking back that foggy night: "I am a lighthouse. You change your course *now!*"

This story is a very close parallel to how I lived my early life. My spiritual journey was very similar to that of the sea captain. I was heading for certain disaster. Then, when I was confronted with the truth about God's incredible love for all of His creation, including me, my course was changed forever.

My name, Adolph Coors, is very familiar to a lot of people. Some have said that the Coors family is the embodiment of the American dream. I don't know if that's accurate, but we did have grand hopes and aspirations, as every family has. The Adolph Coors Company, in Golden, Colorado, has grown into one of the largest breweries in the world.

The Coors Story

The founder, my great-grandfather Adolph Herman Joseph Coors, lost both of his parents at the age of 15. He was trained as a brewer in his native Germany, and in 1868 at the age of 21 he came to America to avoid the German draft. He arrived in this country unable to speak English and with only 17 cents in his pocket. He made his way west and eventually found work as the foreman of a brewery in Naperville, Illinois. By 1872 he had made his way farther west and landed in Denver.

He and a business partner bought an old, abandoned tannery in Golden, about 20 miles west of Denver, where they could start their new brewery. In 1880 his dream was achieved. He bought out his partner and adopted the philosophy, "Never give up and success is attained."

My great-grandfather devoted his entire life to his brewery. His foresight was such that, when Prohibition came to Colorado in 1914, he had already established a pottery company and a bottling operation. Some observers say that America wouldn't have modern porcelain manufacturing had it not been for the vision and ambition of Adolph Coors, Sr. He also began to manufacture malted milk, and soon the Coors company was the third-largest producer of this product in the United States. One of his customers was the growing Mars Candy Company of Chicago.

Years later, on the morning of June 5, 1929, tragedy struck our family. Adolph Coors, Sr., fell to his death from a sixth-story window of a downtown hotel in Virginia Beach, Virginia. The official story was that he had become despondent over problems at the brewery and, after staying up all night with friends, he fell to his death. Was it suicide? Quite likely.

I believe that my great-grandfather learned the same thing that another very prominent man learned many centuries earlier. King Solomon said, "Do not wear yourself out to get rich; have the wisdom to show restraint. Cast but a glance at riches, and they are gone, for they will surely sprout wings and fly off to the sky like an eagle" (Proverbs 23:4,5).

My great-grandfather learned the hard way that wealth, prestige, and power aren't the ultimate source of gratification. They didn't satisfy Solomon, and they didn't satisfy Adolph Coors, Sr.

By the time I arrived on the scene, the Coors family had regained some stability. The first 14 years of my life were like a beautiful Norman Rockwell painting. I was part of a loving, close-knit family with two older sisters, one younger brother, and two fantastic parents. We did everything together.

I remember wanting to grow up to be just like my dad. He was a remarkable man. As a successful businessman he was chairman of the Adolph Coors Co. But he was also a private pilot, multitalented athlete, cattle rancher, and pioneer in the development of skiing in Colorado.

In keeping with our Dutch-German heritage, the father of the family ruled supreme. My father, Adolph Coors III, was the patriarch. But with all of his great accomplishments, the only thing that stands out in my mind about my dad is that, as busy as he was, he always had time to spend with us. He loved us, and he didn't mind showing it. When necessary, he was quite stern, and was very strong on discipline.

However, I regret to say that there was one missing ingredient to this Rockwell painting. Almost every Sunday morning, as a young boy, I found myself in church with my sisters, but I don't remember my mom or dad ever coming with us. They were a vital, but missing ingredient to our Sunday mornings.

"Life Does Not Shout; It Just Runs Out"

When I was 13, my father grew tired of living in the city and moved our family from Denver to our ranch in the foothills west of Denver. He had designed and built our beautiful home, which to me was like the perfect American Dream home.

But, as is true for all families, life brings many changes. Some are sudden, some are gradual. Most are welcome, some bring pain. Tragically, most people place their security in other people. It's a mistake to put our complete trust in our immediate family, our relatives, our friends, and even ourselves. God tells us, "He who fears the LORD has a secure fortress, and for his children it will be a refuge" (Proverbs 14:26). In other words, God tells us to thankfully receive His gifts, but not to put our faith and trust in these gifts. We are to make Him our rock of security.

One tragic day in 1960, the fabric of this wonderful family was violently torn apart. All that was the Coors name, all of our legacy, couldn't protect us. The saying, "Life does not shout; it just runs out, sooner than we think," applied to us.

February 9 was a bitter-cold day, typical for Colorado at that time of year. As usual, my father was up early, ate breakfast alone, and left the house before I saw him. Through the falling snow, he made his way from our ranch to the brewery in Golden, 12 miles away. As he drove down the same road he had traveled countless times before, he noticed a yellow

1958 Mercury parked on a small bridge. Stopping to help, he approached the driver of the car. But the man didn't need assistance. He was waiting for my father. It was a day the man had been planning for two years.

The two men fought. As my father ran back toward his car, the attacker, an escaped prisoner from California, repeatedly shot my father in the back. Alive or dead, my dad's body was stuffed into the trunk of the Mercury and the car sped off. The only clues as to what might have happened were found by a passing milkman two hours later. He found my father's baseball cap and glasses, and blood on the bridge railing. Dad's car, with the motor running, was a few yards away.

Ironically, in 1933 there was a kidnap attempt on my grandfather, Adolph Coors, Jr. The ransom was 50,000 dollars. It was an unfortunate prologue to the kidnapping of his son, my father, 27 years later.

From the day I was born, my life revolved around my father and the Coors family tradition. This event took a turn that exposed me as unprepared. For seven long months after my father's disappearance, we didn't know if he was alive or dead. As the FBI investigated, my mom, sisters, brother, and I all held out that faint hope that Dad would return to his loving family.

But it didn't work out that way. Dad's remains were found near a dump site, 40 miles away. Life does not shout; it just runs out, sooner than we think. When our family got the news that Dad wasn't coming back, I saw my radiantly beautiful mom change before my very eyes. Hatred for the man who brutally murdered her husband began to consume her. Then she turned to alcohol in an attempt to fill the tremendous void and hurt in her heart. She drank to excess, and we kids were powerless to stop her.

I enrolled at a small college in Georgia, but was emotionally unable to handle the responsibility of being on my own. I majored in fraternity and sorority and minored in academics. I lasted one year.

The Age of the Half-Read Page

The next three years I spent in the United States Marine Corps. With the name Adolph Coors, I quickly discovered that if I was going to survive as a Marine, I was going to have to quickly become very tough. I became painfully aware that muscle, brawn, and pride were my only real friends. I was consumed with proving that I was a rougher and tougher Marine than anyone else, and I was committed to not failing in this assignment.

There were a lot of people betting that I wouldn't make it as a Marine. But I was like the saying, "Pride is like a man's shirt—it's the first thing on, and the last thing off." I masked my tremendous insecurity and void by hiding behind the tough, macho Marine image. I became heavily involved in martial arts, and in the next seven years my weight went from 195 pounds to 272 pounds. I hid behind 20" arms and a 54" chest. The saying, "He who falls in love with himself will have no rivals," applied to me.

But God warns us in Proverbs 16:18 that "pride goes before destruction, a haughty spirit before a fall." In other words, be humble or you will tumble. I wouldn't have worried so much about what other people thought of me if I had known how seldom they did!

During this time, one of the things I refused to think about was my own death. Was I ready? Was my passport in order? I didn't care. Even after my older sister, a proud mother of a new baby boy, died of cancer, I continued in my denial of my own life running out.

After the Marine Corps I married my high school sweetheart, B.J. Unfortunately, we spent the first several years together buying things we didn't need, to impress people we didn't like. Our lives were similar to how much of

America lives. We would leap out of bed early in the morning, off and running. We would turn on the radio or TV, brush our teeth, get the coffee going, shower, get dressed, and go to the office. Late in the day we would come home, have dinner, watch some more TV, go to bed, and so on, day after day, week after week, year after year.

I read a poem that described our life:

> This is the age of the half-read page,
> And the quick hash, and the mad dash,
> The bright night, with the nerves tight,
> The plane hop, with the brief stop,
> And the lamp tan in a brief span,
> The big shot, in a good spot,
> And the brain strain, and the heart pain,
> And the cat naps til the spring snaps,
> And the fun's done.

We all know a lot of people who live like that. But Matthew 16:26 asks the important question: "What good will it be for a man if he gains the whole world, yet forfeits his soul? Or what can a man give in exchange for his soul?"

C. S. Lewis, one of the past century's most gifted Christian writers, tells each of us, "If you live for the next world, you get this one in the deal; but if you only live for this world, you end up losing them both."

And the psalmist wrote, "As for man, his days are like grass, he flourishes like a flower of the field; the wind blows over it and it is gone, and its place remembers it no more" (Psalm 103:15,16).

Is any rich person *truly* rich? Henry David Thoreau said that a man is rich in proportion to the number of things he or she can afford to leave alone. In other words, how much money does it take for a rich person to be happy? Just a little more. Thoreau also said, "The masses of mankind lead lives of quiet desperation." That pretty accurately described the lives my wife and I were leading, as well as the lives of most of the people we knew.

The Emptiness of Material Wealth

Life was an endless string of materialistic "if onlys." If only we could get that raise, if only we could get that better-paying job, if only we could get that new car, that new home, that new suit, that new dress...then we would be happy. When lived that way, life is wasted in the endless pursuit of things which, even if attained, will never bring us true and lasting fulfillment.

Most of us fail to recognize that the bait of wealth hides the hook of addiction and eventual slavery to our possessions. John Rockefeller once said, "I have made millions, but they have brought me no happiness." Henry Ford, Sr. once told a friend, "I was happier when I was doing a mechanic's job."

Why were these successful men able to admit that there was something missing in their lives? God created us with "batteries not included." In other words, God has placed a spiritual vacuum in the heart of every human being. It's a vacuum that can't be filled with any created thing. It must be filled by Him or we remain empty.

In the early days of our marriage, B.J. tried to change me into a new person, and I put unfair pressure on her to fill the tremendous void in my heart. I buried myself in materialism, hoping that something would finally give my life some meaning and purpose. I thought owning a mountain home would most certainly be the answer for us, so I purchased a beautiful lake-front home in the mountains west of Denver. Every weekend, always surrounded by friends, we would spend two frantic days trying to be happy.

B.J. and I didn't feel comfortable alone with each other, so we always invited another couple to join us. As long as we were with other people, we didn't have to come to grips with our incompatibility.

I continued trying to carry the burden of the Coors name in the only way I knew how: by striving first for success, then for more and more money. I went to the University of Denver School of Business and set a personal goal of becoming a millionaire by the time I was 30. I had five years to accomplish my goal.

A nagging question kept visiting me, though. "Adolph, why do you feel so empty?" I asked myself over and over. No answer came, so I continued my quest for financial gain. I began to invest heavily in Colorado real estate and in commodity markets in Chicago. I felt that those were the two best vehicles for achieving my goal. Unfortunately, there was an unexpected change in the national economy. Huge losses in real estate and commodities quickly thwarted my plan.

My goal shifted when I joined the family business, the Adolph Coors Company. This time my goal was to become the youngest president in its history. I wanted to follow in the footsteps of my dad, my grandfather, and my great-grandfather, the company founder. Frantically I climbed the corporate ladder, so caught up with what the world defines as success that, in the process, I was destroying those closest to me: my wife and baby son.

In all of this gaining, I was losing. Someone has said that success is getting what you think you want. Happiness is wanting what you get. I was successful but not happy.

Searching for Meaning and Purpose

Then early one October morning, while returning home from work, I suffered a near-fatal car accident. While recovering, I began to take a hard look at my life. I was facing the embarrassment of financial ruin and living in a marriage that was heading for divorce.

I continued to search for the one thing that would lighten my burden and give my life some real meaning and purpose. A lot of people run to the pill bottle, the booze bottle, the affair, the experience, in order to find peace, joy, purpose, and meaning to life. I was one of them.

I asked all of the questions like, Who am I, really? Why am I here? Where am I going? What am I going to do with the rest of my time here? I was experiencing that spiritual vacuum that God has placed in each of us, a vacuum that longs to be filled. St. Augustine, one of the great leaders of the early Christian church, said, "Oh God, you have made us for Yourself, and therefore our souls are restless until they find their rest in You." That was me. My life was in total shambles. I despaired over ever amounting to anything.

Eventually the injuries from the accident healed and I returned to work. But shortly thereafter, my life at the Coors Company took a dramatic turn. I began working for our vice president of administration, who had been hired by my father many years earlier. He had known me most of my life.

One evening B.J. invited this man, Lowell, and his wife, Vera, for dinner. Over that meal Lowell and Vera shared the truth of Jesus Christ with B.J. and me. Through them we learned the truth of John 3:16, that God so loved us—His creation—that He gave His one and only Son, so that anyone who believed in Him would be saved and have eternal life. God Himself took on flesh and blood and came to live with us, in the Person of Jesus Christ.

By their sharing the plan of salvation with us, B.J. and I learned that man is sinful and rebellious, which separates us from God. But we were created to have fellowship with God, and through our self-will, that fellowship had been broken. That separation causes death. Romans 6:23 says, "For the wages of sin is death, but the gift of God is eternal life in Christ Jesus our Lord."

Lowell and Vera explained that Jesus Christ is God's only provision for man's sin. He died on the cross of Calvary in our place. Romans 5:8 says, "But God demonstrates his own love for us in this: While we were still sinners,

Christ died for us." In other words, we broke the law, and Jesus Christ paid the fine. Then B.J. and I learned that we must individually receive Christ as Savior and Lord by a personal invitation. Receiving Christ involved turning from self and trusting Jesus to come into our lives, to forgive our sins, and to make us the kind of persons He created us to be. Lowell and Vera showed us how we had been putting our hope in the wrong things. The foundation of our lives was wishful thinking.

A few days later B.J. invited Jesus Christ to come into her life. The void she had been experiencing was immediately filled. When she made that decision, I saw a dramatic change in her life. Deep down, I knew that she had found the one thing that I desperately needed. But I still wasn't ready to give up the struggle. Pride is the only disease that makes everyone sick except the one who has it.

It wasn't long after this that my wife and I agreed to a separation. Our marriage hadn't been going well, and I saw no improvement ahead, so I moved out, leaving B.J. and my three-year-old son, Shane. During those painful weeks of separation from my family, I began to listen for the first time to what God was so clearly saying to me. For years I had shut my mind to Him. I had been running so hard from God. But I couldn't continue that way.

I was, at long last, coming to the end of myself. When you finally realize you're nobody special, you quit worrying about making a comeback. And apart from God, I was a nobody.

I began reading a book Lowell gave me called *Do Yourself a Favor: Love Your Wife* by H. Page Williams. In this book, I learned the importance of applying God's priorities to my life. Mine obviously weren't working. The most important priority was a personal, ongoing relationship with my heavenly Father. Second, I needed to love my wife with the selfless *agape* love that can only come from God. Feelings come and go, and true love can't be based on something so transitory. It has to be based on commitment. Third, I needed to develop a close relationship with my son. That wouldn't come unless I was willing to devote quality time to that relationship. Last, the book showed me that I needed to cultivate true friends. True friends are like diamonds, precious but rare; false friends are like autumn leaves, found everywhere.

Changing Course

One afternoon, while still separated from my family, I went to hear a man speak in downtown Denver. As I sat in the auditorium, surrounded by hundreds of people, his words deeply penetrated my heart. He quoted Acts 4:12: "Salvation is found in no one else, for there is no other name under heaven given to men by which we must be saved." Later that day, by an act of my will, I opened my heart and life to Jesus Christ. I said a simple prayer, and as I did, Jesus filled the void that I had tried to fill for nearly 30 years. The truth of God's unconditional love began to flood my entire being. I had never experienced that kind of love. Suddenly, the one thing I had been looking for was finally mine.

The things that had been so important to me no longer were. For the first time, my marriage to B.J. and my relationship with my son took their proper place in my list of priorities. My ship was changing course. B.J. and I agreed to make our marriage work. We discovered that a good marriage is a union of two forgivers. I was beginning to learn that love is not only finding the right person, it's also being the right person.

It was important for me to realize that this new relationship with Christ wasn't just a belief in a religion. Religion won't do anyone any good. It's nothing more than a feeble attempt to cross a barrier that separates a person from God. This simply won't work, because the Bible makes it clear that man's righteousness is inadequate for his salvation. No work of man can ever tear down the barrier that separates us from God. Remember, "For all have sinned and fall short of the glory of God" (Romans 3:23). The only way to tear down this barrier is through faith in Jesus Christ. That's based on the words in Acts 16:31: "Believe in the Lord Jesus, and you will be saved."

This isn't a religion; it's a relationship. God doesn't love us because of who we are or what we can do. That's religion. God loves us because of who He is and what He has already done.

B.J. and I shared our good news with my mother just before she was leaving for a short vacation. Mom was interested as we told her how she could invite Jesus into her life. After a brief but meaningful conversation with both of us, she departed for her trip, and promised to call us when she returned. But three days later, Mom suffered a major stroke. A few hours later, she died. Life does not shout; it just runs out, sooner than we think.

Forgiving the Unforgivable

Even though I had accepted Christ, there was still one area that gave me tremendous trouble. I had developed an intense hatred for the man who brutally murdered my dad. The FBI had arrested him in Vancouver, British Columbia, and brought him back to Colorado, where he was sentenced to life in the Colorado State Penitentiary.

I hated this man. But hatred is like a treacherous acid, which cannot be poured without spilling on the raw heart that held it. I can speak from experience that hate hurts the hater far more than the person being hated.

Jesus Christ began to impress on me the need to forgive the man who killed my dad. I tried on countless occasions, but I wasn't able to do it. If forgiveness was going to come at all, it was going to have to come from a source higher than me. But

I soon realized that if anyone had a right to hate, it was Jesus Christ. While suffering the horrible agonies of crucifixion, the most hideous form of execution devised by man, our Savior looked down from the cross at the soldiers who nailed Him there and said, "Father, forgive them, for they do not know what they are doing" (Luke 23:34).

I remembered, too, that despite all of my sin, Jesus loved me enough to go to the cross and die for me. Romans 5:8 says, "But God demonstrates his own love for us in this: While we were still sinners, Christ died for us." As I began to comprehend this beautiful truth, it became painfully obvious that I had no right to hate another human being—not even the man who murdered my wonderful dad. The need to forgive involved a decision on my part. But I knew that I wasn't capable of that kind of forgiveness. But by searching in God's Word, I found my answer in Philippians 4:13: "I can do everything through him who gives me strength."

Finally, with the help of a friend who regularly visits inmates to share Christ with them, I went to see my dad's killer. Three separate times he refused to see me. So I wrote him a note, asking for his forgiveness for the hatred that I had in my heart for him for so many years. I also said that I forgave him for the pain and suffering he had caused my family and me.

As I was obedient to what Jesus Christ asked me to do through His Word, He did what I could never have done for myself. He removed the hatred from my heart that had burned there for so long. In its place He put a love that could only come from Him. The process of true and complete forgiveness can only begin with Jesus in your heart—not before.

My life had been set on a course of destruction. I was destroying myself and those I loved. The message that was beamed to me through God's Word and through His servants was that I needed to change course or I would crash. I kept giving the signals back, saying, "Get out of my way." I am so grateful that I got the message before it was too late.

The lesson of my life is that we all need to pay attention to the lighthouse of God. We Christians are like lighthouse keepers who are there to direct other people to pay attention to the light. We're the ones sending the signals to those in the world who believe they can manage on their own. The world needs more people like Lowell and Vera, who can beam a message of hope to people who are headed for destruction, whose lives are running out the way mine was.

Will you be in the lighthouse for Jesus?

I was first introduced to Vince D'Acchioli about seven years ago. A good friend recommended Vince as an excellent resource and motivational speaker. Over the years, I have come to know Vince both as a personal friend and as an effective leader in the Christian community.

Vince is the founder of On Target Ministries, a ministry dedicated to helping men, couples, and pastors discover God's plan for their life. This dynamic outreach continues to encourage thousands of men and women across the United States and Canada to reach toward and ultimately fulfill their spiritual potential.

Vince's experience as corporate vice president for a major Fortune 1000 company, combined with his stint as an executive vice president for an international ministry, has uniquely equipped him with a relevant and well-balanced message for all of us. You will find his humorous, laid-back style refreshing and engaging.

Vince and his wife, Cindy, married 35 years, have two daughters and reside in Colorado Springs, Colorado. Vince is also the author of *Wired to Work,* published by Huntington House.

6

Getting Past Superficiality

Vince D'Acchioli

AS I TRAVEL THROUGHOUT THE UNITED States and Canada speaking to groups, I often ask the question, "How many of you are satisfied with our modern culture? How many think we are headed in the right direction?" The response is minimal. The next question I ask is, "If you had to lay the blame for our condition anywhere, where would you place it?" A lot of people respond by pointing to the government, political leaders, educational institutions, and the media.

While all these are powerful and oftentimes negative influences, I believe that the real blame for our condition belongs squarely at the foot of the church of Jesus Christ. God intended for His followers to act as beacons, shedding light in a world of darkness. We must begin to take that responsibility seriously.

Suppose you were to ask a radical feminist, "Tell me the first thing that comes to mind when I say the words *evangelical Christian man.*" What do you think her response might be? I don't know what she would say, but I can tell you what she *wouldn't* say. She would not say, "Those are the kind of men who know how to love and cherish a woman. Those are the kind of men every woman should meet."

What if I were to ask a man caught in a homosexual lifestyle, "Tell me the first thing that comes to mind when I say the words *evangelical Christian.*" While responses may vary, I'm pretty sure that he wouldn't say, "While they don't agree with my lifestyle, I've never felt such love and compassion. They are building and running our hospices. They're always there to pray for us in our time of need."

What if you were to walk up to a board member for the National Education Association and ask, "What's the first thing that comes to mind when I say the words *evangelical Christian?*" It's not likely that you would hear, "Those parents have the kids we want in our schools. They're the parents we want to have on our boards. They're incredibly encouraging and supportive." We will never win this nation for Jesus as long as these kinds of reactions prevail.

Most people are familiar with the famous painting of the Mona Lisa. But how many could describe its frame? The reason no one can remember the frame is because the job of a good frame is to complement its contents, not to draw attention to itself. In light of this illustration, what are people seeing when they look at you and me? Are they seeing Jesus, or are they seeing the frame of our humanness? I pray that they're seeing who we've been called to exemplify: Jesus Christ.

Growing Up "Ethnically Advantaged"

Allow me to apply this illustration to my own life. I was born into a very large Italian family in Rhode Island, where the politically correct term for *Italian* is *ethnically advantaged*. To us, everyone else is ethnically challenged. Where I grew up, the rule was that everyone who was anyone had to be Italian, Catholic, and Democrat. You also learned to play the accordion by age four.

My family moved to southern California when I was eight. My parents said we were going on a two-week vacation, which, to my brother and sister and me, was an extravagance we couldn't imagine. Little did we know that we would never return to our home state. I found out later that my father had run into some financial trouble and was intent on making a new start.

After settling into our new home, my parents enrolled me in Catholic school. I wasn't a very disciplined boy, so I was frequently in trouble with the brothers and sisters who taught at the school. In tenth grade I was flunked out of high school with four Fs and a D. For a long time I was proud to state that the D was in religion.

At the age of 13, I acquired a part-time job at Standard Brands Paint Company sweeping floors and stocking shelves. Between work and family, I had some pretty awful role models. At work I learned all the wrong ideals: how to stay out late, chase women, and drink to excess. At home, I learned a lot about life from my Uncle Louie. I know it sounds like a cliché for a guy from a big Italian family to have an Uncle Louie, but I did!

Uncle Louie and I would often hang out in the bars together. Many times we were joined by the same group of guys. They were FBI men who had been assigned to watch my uncle. Uncle Lou was always aware of their presence and even made casual conversation at times. I thought that was cool. Even when playing golf he was being watched by helicopter.

The only thing that kept me from getting sucked into that same lifestyle was falling in love. Cindy and I were high school sweethearts and were married shortly after graduation. But in tying the knot so very quickly, we had unknowingly set the stage for disaster.

Trouble on the Homefront

With the added financial responsibility of marriage, I began to work 40 hours a week at the paint store and enrolled in college part-time. During this time I remember visiting my mother-in-law's house. Cindy's younger brother excitedly shared the news that he had just accepted Jesus Christ at a Campus Crusade for Christ meeting. He couldn't stop talking about his "born again" experience. His conversion deeply affected Cindy. I didn't know it at the time, but she had been quietly seeking the Lord for several months. When she saw the joy on her brother's face (a fellow who had previously been caught growing marijuana in the family birdbath), she knew the change was real. Shortly thereafter, Cindy made her own personal commitment to the Lord. All I asked was that she leave me out of it.

From that moment on, our lives headed in opposite directions at an accelerated pace. Friends counseled Cindy to abandon the marriage. One person asked her why she stayed with me, because it was obvious that I would never become a Christian. But as time went by, I began to notice some changes in Cindy's life. Out of sheer curiosity, I agreed to accompany her to a Wednesday night Bible study at an old fraternity house near the UCLA campus.

The frat house was packed with young people, and we struggled to find a place on the floor to sit. There was a lot of energy and excitement in the air. Before long, a tall, rough-looking man, wearing a black leather jacket, opened the meeting with his testimony. He told of his connection to the Mafia and his years with the Hell's Angels motorcycle gang. Then he told how accepting Christ had changed his life. He completely blew my stereotype of what a Christian was. Then a man named Hal Lindsay spoke. He made the Bible come alive! As a result, seeds were sown, but I wasn't ready to let them take root.

Jesus as Savior, But Not Lord

A few months later, on my commute home from work, I took some time to reflect on my life. I had just been promoted to store manager in Pasadena. My company stock was booming, and I was in line for another promotion. My outlook was as bright as the sunny southern California climate. However, I had an overwhelming sense that if I didn't get serious about God right at that moment, I might never have a second chance. As I sat in bumper-to-bumper traffic that afternoon, I prayed my version of the sinner's prayer: "Lord, if You are real, I want the kind of relationship with You that these other people have."

When I got home, I proudly announced what I had done to Cindy. She was thrilled! She remembered the wonderful effect conversion had on her brother's life, and couldn't wait to see the evidence of change in mine. Sadly, Cindy's optimism was soon crushed. Although I professed to be a believer, my life didn't change. I didn't read the Bible, pray, or attend church. What I did was accept Jesus as my Savior but not as my Lord. There's a big difference.

During the next eight years I did more damage in the kingdom of God as a new believer than before I knew God!

At work I was promoted to district manager. Along with the title came responsibility for more than a dozen stores and hundreds of employees. The new position also required a lot of travel and, as is often the case, the time spent apart from my family soon gave way to temptations. My new executive lifestyle included drinking and adultery. My employees knew that I was a Christian, and yet they were also aware of my lifestyle. I could hear them in the back room saying, "What a hypocrite." Followers of Christ must realize that they're constantly being watched.

Eventually, Cindy uncovered my secrets. It was the first predicament that I couldn't manipulate myself out of. A pastor friend of mine always used to say, "There is no such thing as a secret." How true that is. I was dangerously close to losing the people I loved most in my life: my wife and my children.

"You Told Him, Didn't You?"

Over the next week or so Cindy and I didn't communicate much. Cindy waited on the Lord and sensed God telling her, "Be still and quiet. I am wrestling with Vince's soul." At the time, she and the kids had been attending the Church on the Way in Van Nuys, California. One Sunday, in an effort to find marital and spiritual healing, I decided to join them. About halfway through Pastor Hayford's piercing sermon, I turned to Cindy and said, "You told him, didn't you?" It was as if every word he spoke was directed to me.

After the sermon, Pastor Hayford asked the congregation to form small prayer circles. When one of the guys in my group asked if I had a request, I let it all out. I thought that they would all be flabbergasted. Instead, they listened quietly and then prayed over me. It was incredible. I didn't know anything about the ways of the Lord back then, but the Holy Spirit was doing unbelievable things.

Soon after, Cindy and I began attending counseling sessions with one of the associate pastors. In the first appointment we poured out our hearts and then waited for the counselor's response. He paused, then turned to Cindy and asked, "What are you going to do?"

"I don't know," Cindy replied.

"What did Jesus do for you?" asked the pastor.

Cindy's response came immediately. "He went to the cross."

"Then what?"

Cindy paused, then answered, "He died."

The counselor's next words reverberate in my mind even today. He turned to me and said, "Vince, I want you to look into your wife's eyes." I did so for an uncomfortable amount of time. What he said to me next cut me to my core: "I don't see much life in there, do you?"

In that moment, God gave me a panoramic view of the incredible amount of hurt and pain that I had heaped upon this precious child of His. I can't remember a time when I ever felt so ashamed. I repented for my sins and was incredibly grateful when my wife agreed to stay and work things out. She told me later that God whispered to her in a clear but inaudible voice, "If you will forgive Vince, I promise you there will be a third-day resurrection."

A New Man

I was baptized soon after this event, and Christ reached down and washed me clean. He stripped away all of my guilt and condemnation. For the very first time, I was finally able to let go of my past. I felt like a new man! With a newfound sense of conviction, I made a habit of studying the Bible and incorporating God's Word into my life. The Lord became my "spiritual CEO."

Things at work took off as well. After 13 years at the company, I was named corporate vice president. But before long the company's business philosophies began to change. In an effort to avoid a hostile takeover, several of us met on the top floor of a Los Angeles skyscraper with scores of lawyers, bankers, accountants, and company executives to sign for a 200-million-dollar loan. The interest payments alone were staggering. At that moment, we made some serious mistakes as leaders. My life was like the movie *Wall Street*.

In the midst of all this turmoil, I remember praying, "Lord, You must have something else for me." After much time in prayer, God led me to a Christian man who happened to be looking for an executive vice president to help him merge with another ministry.

As a businessman I had been used to dealing with blacks, whites, Jews, Greeks, Italians, and everyone else, but every management tool I possessed was worthless when it came to trying to get two religious cultures to come together! It was ugly, and I learned how helpless I was. The only useful and effective weapon was prayer.

Superficial Christianity

After several years of service with this ministry, I felt that my position there was no longer necessary. I began to ask what God had in store for me next. While waiting, I took stock of the culture around me. I noticed the direction our country was heading and felt a sense of deep sadness over our condition. Where do you think most of the pornography sent around the world on the Internet comes from? We export it. Most of the garbage in the entertainment media is created right here in the United States.

How did this happen? This may sound like a bold statement, but I believe we've produced the most superficial Christianity the world has ever known. In business, our goal was to develop a product that would satisfy our customer. We found out what the customer needed and made a product to satisfy that need. And isn't that what the church so often does too? We shouldn't be changing our behavior to satisfy our culture. As a result of our buying into this business mentality, we have watered down our faith. What does it mean to be a Christian anymore?

Please understand, I'm not suggesting that all Christians are guilty of this, but when we think of the body of Christ in this country, we tend to think in narrow terms like our own church congregation or denomination. But the body of Christ encompasses a multitude! The number of people who profess Jesus as their Lord and Savior is enormous!

Let me share an experience with you that may reveal something we're all missing. While speaking to a group of pastors recently, I asked the following question: "Pastors, tell me, what is your *product?*" I could tell that some of them were a little intimidated by my use of business terminology. I explained that my question wasn't meant to address them personally, but rather the broader aspect of the church. In other words, if the church were a factory, what would its product be?

Many of these men had a difficult time articulating a response. Finally, after a few minutes had passed, I initiated a second question. "What is Chrysler's product?" The immediate response was "cars." I then suggested that while it is true that they assemble cars, they are not really their product. As confusion began to break out, I continued, "Chrysler's product is really transportation. They manufacture cars to satisfy a wide range of transportation needs."

The pastors seemed to readily accept this notion. I then restated my first question. "So, using this illustration, what is *your* product?" One gentleman readily answered, "The product of the local church is to produce *Christlike people*." What a great response! We should be producing people who truly reflect Jesus. However, aren't Christlike people really like the car?

You see, I believe that the product of the church ought to be *a godly world*. It would follow then that the product of a church in Colorado Springs ought to be a godly Colorado Springs. I wanted these pastors to see the big picture. Just as Chrysler remembers each time they manufacture a car that their purpose is to satisfy and provide transportation needs, we as the church need to recognize that the purpose of building up Christlike people is to produce godliness in a hurting world.

I continued my teaching that day with a challenging question: "Most of us would agree that Chrysler is doing a pretty good job in delivering a quality product. Now tell me, how do you think the church is doing?" After a brief time of reflection, I followed with this final illustration:

> Let's assume that Chrysler has gone out and purchased the best raw materials available. At this point, they could throw all of this rubber, glass, metal, plastic, etc. into a box on the factory floor and call it a car. Clearly, we would never identify this box of parts as a car. It could never lead to transportation. Now I want you to think of an average man or woman sitting in church receiving the

greatest raw material the world has ever known. Not since Jesus walked the planet have we been equipped with such extraordinary wisdom and knowledge. To think that this human being will step out of that building a Christlike person is as ludicrous as believing that a box of parts is a car.

So how should we go about solving this problem? Chrysler figured out a system that we as the body of Christ should consider and employ. First, they went to the drawing board and asked themselves an important question: "What is this car supposed to look like?" Then they drew up every detail. With a clear vision in mind, they initiated an assembly line. They realized that they could not attach the wheel before the axle, or the engine before the frame. (It's interesting that in the academic community we know that you do not teach advanced calculus to a first grader, yet somehow we have lost that concept when trying to develop Christlike people.) For Chrysler, the work is done part upon part; for us it should be done precept upon precept.

In continuing their process, Chrysler does not stop at the assembly line. They do not want to take any chances. Before one of their cars is allowed to leave the factory, they send a person with a clipboard down to the end of the line. This person is required to give the car a thorough inspection. Then they go to the check box on top of the form that asks, "Is this product ready to represent our company?" If the answer is yes, a check goes in the box and the car is out the door.

When people at my company looked at me during my days of sinning, they didn't see someone who looked like Jesus. They saw someone who proclaimed Christianity, but who walked and talked

> just like everyone else in the world. There ought to be evidence that the church is doing its job. We need to integrate a stronger disciple-building process in our churches. We bring people to Jesus, but then what? Where's the depth?

In my opinion we aren't doing a very good job of framing Jesus. We allow our superficiality to get in the way. So how did we get here? The answer became clearer to me when I met a woman by the name of Betsy Sanders. Betsy, in her late thirties at the time, had worked her way up from a sales associate to executive vice president for Nordstrom department stores in the Pacific Northwest. Betsy told a story at an event I attended that so caught my attention that I asked her if she would come to my company and share it with our executive team. She agreed and this is the story she told:

One day a group of executives from Nordstrom invited a number of top executives from J.C. Penney to a luncheon. They were all seated around a large table enjoying their meal when one of the executives from J.C. Penney asked the following question: "To what do you attribute your tremendous success? Nordstrom has become a model that people all over the world are studying." What he was basically looking for was the key to their success.

The way I remember Betsy telling it, one of the executives from Nordstrom excused himself for a few moments in order to retrieve a large book from an adjacent room. He brought the book over to the Penney's executive, opened it, and laid it in front of him. The book, written 100 years ago, was the original operational manual for J.C. Penney. He simply said, "We do everything that it says in this book."

What an uncomfortable moment that must have been for that team from J.C. Penney. You see, what the executive from Nordstrom was really trying to communicate was that

J.C. Penney had lost their "first love." They had the *vision* and somewhere along the way they allowed it to slip away. Sadly, this is what happens in the lives of many organizations, churches, marriages, and individuals.

Consulting the Owner's Manual

The answer lies in rediscovering what God's vision is for us personally. And I believe there's only one way to accomplish this. It's by becoming intimate with our heavenly Father. You can't be intimate with someone unless you spend some time alone with that person. I used to convince myself that I had done my spiritual duty for God by going to church. Coming together with a community of believers is necessary for spiritual growth, but it should never take the place of our time alone with God.

So what should we do during that time alone? One thing we need to do is read His Word. Joshua 1:8 says, "Do not let this Book of the Law depart from your mouth; meditate on it day and night." Matthew 22:29 says, "Jesus replied, 'You are in error because you do not know the Scriptures or the power of God.'"

Most of us have computers in our homes, all of which arrived with a healthy-sized owner's manual. The original writer of the programs knew that we wouldn't be able to figure everything out, so it was written down in a book for our use. But if you're anything like me, you don't need that silly manual—you can figure it out all by yourself.

In my house the manual ended up on the top shelf, next to my Bible. And for a while everything worked just fine. That is, until I wanted to try something more difficult. Soon I was staring at a blue screen covered with error messages.

Immediately I called for technical support, and my conversation went something like this:

"How can I help you?"

"Well, I'm using this program and it just isn't doing what I'm asking it to do."

"What is it doing, sir?"

"I'm asking it to do a, b, and c, and it's responding with x, y, and z."

"Sir, do you happen to have your manual handy?"

"Yeah. Let me pull it down off the shelf."

"Okay, now turn to page 974. Do you see the illustration at the top of the page? Is that what your computer is doing?"

"Yes. That's exactly what's happening."

"Do you see the instructions just below that diagram?"

"Yes."

"If you follow the instructions provided, you will avoid having that problem again."

Can this illustration be applied to our lives? You bet! Just like that computer, we have been manufactured. Someone wrote our code and knows exactly how every part of our program is supposed to function. Then He placed us on earth and provided us with a manual: the Bible. But oftentimes we treat it the same way we treat our computer manual. We don't refer to it until we're in trouble. But the truth is, as Psalm 119:105 says, "Your word is a lamp to my feet and a light for my path." If we choose to live in God's Word, it will illuminate our daily walk.

There is no way we will ever discover God's vision or have the ability to live it out unless we are intimate with Him. We are mired in our superficial approach to Christianity because we refuse to get serious about our relationship with God.

Six Principles

Reading God's Word is just one way to grow more intimate with Him. Another is to spend time alone in prayer. Allow me to share with you what I call "The Six Principles for Effective Prayer":

1. *Schedule it.* If you don't schedule it, you won't do it. I read a book many years ago titled *Eckerd.* In his autobiography, Jack Eckerd talks about how he would go to work every morning and retreat directly to his office. From about 7:30 to 8:30 A.M. he would schedule a time alone with God. Jack protected that hour as though it was the most significant meeting of the day. What a great example of how we should be treating our intimate moments with the Father.

2. *Find a quiet place.* This may be your office, a study, your basement, or a place in your home where there is little family traffic. Some people have even designated a special room or closet in their home especially for the purpose of prayer. Wherever it may be, be sure to create a private prayer haven of your very own. If you don't have a quiet place, you will never be able to achieve number three: a quiet mind.

3. *Quiet your mind.* This is the greatest challenge for me. It is tough to get my mind into a place of neutral where I am not thinking about anything else but God. To get there, I generally start by praising Him. Then I thank Him and honor Him. Before you know it, everything that was previously clouding your thoughts will fall away and your focus will be on Jesus alone.

4. *Seek Him first—not what you want.* If your mind is quiet and you are truly operating with a heart of praise, it will only be natural to seek God's face rather than His hand. I do not mean to say that it is wrong to bring your petitions before the Lord. The Word clearly instructs us to cast all of our cares on Him. However, it is important that we learn to seek the Giver of the gift before we seek the gift. First seek...then ask!

5. *Ask for His will in all matters.* His plan is perfect and right for every circumstance. If we pray for God's will, we should never be disappointed with the outcome. We can rejoice knowing that He will answer our petition in His own way and in His own time.

6. *Pray against the forces that are at cross-purposes with God's will.* As a result of Jesus' death on the cross and His shed blood, you and I have been given the authority to pray against all forces that are at cross-purposes with God's will. What are those forces? There are three: the world, the flesh, and the devil.

The Importance of Praise

There is one other necessary element to growing more intimate with God. It happens when we praise Him. Praise is one of the most often-mentioned concepts in the entire Bible, yet we don't invest much time in it.

Several years ago, when I was that new superficial believer I talked about earlier, Cindy and I attended a marriage retreat. We sat in the back of the room. Cindy was in the last pew, and I was standing behind her, trying to ease some of the tension out of her neck. The pastor began to preach about the necessity for husbands and wives to encourage each other more often. I remember thinking, "You know, he's right. Cindy doesn't encourage me enough. I hope she's listening to this." The truth be known, I didn't deserve much encouragement in those days. Still, I continued to complain to God. "I hope you're convicting Cindy's heart. She never encourages me. She never lifts me up. She never praises me." As soon as I finished that last thought, God said to me, "I know the feeling." Those words hit me like a dagger. "Get your eyes off Cindy and begin to praise Me."

Over time, I have learned that God's voice is always heard the clearest during moments of intense praise. Second Chronicles 5:13 states, "The trumpeters and singers joined in unison, as with one voice, to give praise and thanks to the LORD. Accompanied by trumpets, cymbals and other instruments, they raised their voices in praise to the LORD and sang, 'He is good; his love endures forever.'" The verse continues, "Then [*then* is a transitional word meaning "as a result of what has just taken place, here is what happened"] the temple of the LORD was filled with a cloud." The cloud, of course, was God's presence. Under the old covenant, God would reside in physical locations: the temple, tabernacle, or ark.

Under the new covenant, 2 Chronicles 5:13 has a whole different connotation. Where does God reside today? In our hearts, right? Wow, what a promise! As the direct result of praising our God, He blesses us with His very presence. Scripture tells us that the Lord inhabits the praises of His people.

A Message for Cindy

I would like to share one final story with you. Some time ago, I drove up to the mountains by myself to fast and pray for my wife. I had just left my position as vice president for a Fortune 1000 company to enter into the world of ministry. My new job required that Cindy and I leave our home in California and relocate to Colorado Springs, Colorado. In doing so, we left behind our home (the home that Cindy had originally grown up in), all of our relatives, and an abundance of dear friends.

Upon arriving in Colorado, we immediately took on the overwhelming project of building a new house. Are you tired yet? The story gets better! Shortly after we settled into our new place, our daughter Kimberly decided to surprise us with the news of her engagement! Within a very short time, we had experienced a major career change, a relocation, the task of building a new home, and the planning of a wedding! The impact was devastating to Cindy, and she was left emotionally drained. This is when I decided to retreat to the mountains to fast and pray for three days on her behalf.

My first day up at that cabin was miserable. My room was void of any modern-day conveniences. There was no phone and no television. After unpacking, I began to pray and ask the Lord to speak to me. I was disappointed when there was no response. That entire first day God did not communicate one thing to me. I was starting to get discouraged. I felt spiritually dry.

It was not until midway through the second day that I began to hear God's voice. What He spoke was delivered to me in three sets of four words. I immediately knew that it was Him. As I continued to pray for Cindy, I received the first set of words. God said to tell Cindy, *"I love you, Cindy."* I must admit that I was a bit disappointed. That seemed too simple. I was ready to jot down some profound theological point with 14 subpoints!

As I began to pray again, the Lord spoke to me a second time. He instructed me to tell Cindy, *"My plans are good."* "Okay, Lord, that is nice, but when are you going to give me some real meat? Your Word tells me that Your plans are for good and not for evil and that we might have a future and a hope. I'm looking for some new material here." I was actually quoting Bible verses to God!

After another hour had passed, I received the last set of four words. The Lord said to tell Cindy, *"Stay close to Me."* That was it! He was done talking! The next day came and was as spiritually dry as the first. I had invested three days in fasting and prayer for three simple sets of four words! I felt like a failure as I drove home with those 12 little words on a small notepad. What was I going to tell Cindy? I was sure that she was expecting so much more.

Still whining, I pulled into the driveway, and Cindy immediately came bolting out of the door into the garage. She seemed so happy to see me. "Welcome home!" she said. "I've had the most wonderful time with God over the last three days. I can't wait to hear what God has said to you." I started to feel my stomach knot up as I thought about how I was going to milk these three sets of four words. Eventually, I pulled the small sheet of notepaper from my pocket and began to read what the Lord had shared. As I did, Cindy began to cry. I thought to myself, *Man, am I in trouble. What? Was it something I said?* Most of us guys are clueless when our wives cry—we don't know what's going on. Then the most amazing thing happened. Through her tears Cindy said, "That is the most fantastic thing I have ever heard. That is exactly what God shared with me. He directed me to it in the Word." Wow! I went from a zero to a hero in just a matter of seconds—and was still as clueless as ever!

The following week I was invited to speak at a staff chapel for a large ministry in Colorado Springs. My audience was primarily made up of evangelical Christians. For about 45 minutes I delivered a teaching that was based on the three sets of four words that I just shared. By the time I was done speaking, people were weeping all around the room. How could such a simple message penetrate the hearts of so many?

It all comes down to what God is speaking to you and to me:

I don't care what your friends think about you.

I don't care what your neighbors think about you.

I don't care what the people at work think about you.

I don't care what your family or the people in your church think about you.

In fact, I don't even care what you think about you.

I love you!

I don't care where you have been or what you have done.

Yes, I know about that dirty magazine—those drugs.

I know about how you are thinking about the man or woman at work.

I know about the affair—the failures.

I know how broken you think you are.

But I sent My Son, Jesus, to die on a cross for you—to once and for all draw a line in the sand that separates you from your past.

My plans are good!

Now here is the key....The secret to understanding God's unconditional love for us and His great plan for our lives lies in this third set of words:

Stay close to Me!

If I could put all of this into one winning formula, it would be: *Intimacy with God = Strength of Vision.* Once we decide to get serious about our relationship with God and allow Him to create depth among us, our lives will change and our nation will be transformed. It's time for the superficiality to end and a new level of intimacy with God to begin.

In the summer of 1989 I asked Bill McCartney, then the head football coach at the University of Colorado, to speak at a Fellowship of Christian Athletes fund-raising banquet in southern California. He agreed, in spite of suffering from a bad case of back pain, and he gave one of the most inspiring messages I've ever heard.

The next morning as I was taking him to the airport, he said he would really like me to pray for a special men's group that he and Dave Wardell were trying to get started. I asked him what they were going to call the group, and he said they didn't have a name yet.

As he was getting out of my car, I gave him a *High Ground and Associates* newspaper that we had put together so he could read it on the plane. Two weeks later Bill called to say that one of the articles in the paper had given him the name for their new men's group. It was going to be called "Promise Keepers."

In 1994, Bill resigned from a lifetime contract, one of the first ones ever signed by a major university, after having coached his team to a national championship in 1990. He was the number-one coach in the country according to all of the polls.

A reasonable person would ask, "Why would anybody resign a lifetime, no-cut contract?" Bill's simple explanation was, "When your job gets in the way of your family and you're about to lose the two most important women in your life—your daughter and your wife—then you have to get your priorities in order and resign from the job. When I realized that coaching had, in part, served to remove the splendor from my wife, Lyndi, I set out to restore that splendor."

Since beginning Promise Keepers in 1994, Bill has spoken widely to men about their roles as husbands and fathers. He is also the author of *Sold Out* and *From Ashes to Glory.* Bill and Lyndi make their home in Colorado.

7

Seeking God's Heart

Bill McCartney

THE GREATEST LONGING OF THE HUMAN spirit is significance. We can spend our whole lives searching for that one thing that makes our lives worthwhile, and yet if we don't find it, we feel lost, useless, meaningless.

I learned this when I was coaching football at the University of Colorado. During one of my last seasons, we were about halfway through our schedule, and we were undefeated. I was feeling pretty good about my coaching job.

It was a Tuesday afternoon and we had just started practice. To get to our practice facility, the team has to exit the locker room, go down a steep embankment for about 110 yards, then go across a gravel parking lot for another 50 yards. The facility is three grass practice fields. The gate into the facility is at the first field, and this particular day I was on the third field, working with our offensive linemen.

We were about 20 minutes into a drill when, from field two, one of the student managers called out, "Coach Mac, you have a phone call."

First of all, the phone is way back up in the locker room, and furthermore, practice was going on. This hadn't happened to me before, and I thought that it was a good opportunity to make a statement to the players about priorities. I said, "Hey, I don't take phone calls during practice." I didn't think I could have been clearer to my players about the importance of the task at hand.

The student yelled back at me, "Coach, it's *Sports Illustrated.*"

You know, I thought, *maybe I ought to take this one.* So I had to eat crow as I started across that field. I started to think about what they might want to write about or talk about. I decided I knew what it was. They had written some mean things over the years, and they wanted to apologize. They had repented. By the time I got to that steep embankment, I thought about our great team—maybe we would win the national championship. We were ranked third or fourth at the time, and they were going to write about this great team we had.

But by the time I had gotten up to the building, I thought no, this column was going to be about me. They had discovered the genius that I was. By the time I got to the phone, I decided I was going to be on the cover of the next issue. So I picked up the phone and said, "Hello, this is Bill McCartney."

A very stilted voice came over the line and said, "Mr. McCartney, this is *Sports Illustrated* in Chicago."

"Yes, sir," I said. "How can I help you?"

"Mr. McCartney, your subscription has expired," was the terse reply.

They had gotten me again, and I confess that I never did renew that subscription!

A Heart for God

Even though I felt pretty insignificant that day, I have discovered where true significance lies. It's in seeking and finding the very heart of God.

Think about this: In every area of life, someone has an advantage over you. Some people have greater intellect. Some people have a greater economic base. Some people are more physically imposing. Some people are more physically attractive. Some people are the right color. Some people have a background they can draw on.

But in God's wisdom, there's one area where no one has an advantage—not even an inch—and it's the one area that's the most important. God has said, "You shall seek Me and you shall find Me when you seek Me with all of your heart."

It doesn't matter what color you are, what sex, what size, what your background is—it doesn't matter. Do you want God's heart? That's all that matters. And anyone who wants the heart of God can have it. When we have it, our lives take on full meaning and purpose.

Have you ever thought about the fact that there are a lot of Christians who are unhappy? They know Jesus, they pray to Him, they're trying to live as He lived. So why aren't they hitting on all cylinders? Because they haven't gone after the heart of God with all of themselves.

What does a tree do? It gives oxygen, fruit, and shade. What does the sun do? It marks the calendar, separates day and night. It lights the earth. Just as all of God's creation has a special, significant purpose, so does every individual person. When we enter into that pursuit of the heart of God, that's when we're capable of living in our highest purpose and when we find true significance.

Everyone knows that water at 211° is plenty hot. But at 212° it boils. At 211°, a steam engine cannot move a freight train. But at 212° the engine can pull a mile-long train around a mountain pass. One degree makes a tremendous difference in a steam engine. It's the same thing if we turn up a degree in how we go after the heart of God. If we get rid of the things that clutter us and separate us and demand our time and our thoughts, and we start going after His heart every chance we get, that's what I mean by taking it up a degree.

Why did Jesus pray for 40 days and 40 nights? He wanted God's heart. He was after the very heart of God. He was the Son of God and He craved intimate fellowship with the Father. In his thirst for His Father's heart, Jesus set an example for us.

My Awakening to Racial Pain

For me, this desire to take things up a degree or two started in the 1980s. Back then I was consumed, driven, obsessed, and possessed by coaching football. In the late 1980s we had a young black attorney in Denver by the name of Teddy Woods. Teddy was about 40 when he died suddenly, tragically, of a heart attack. I didn't know him very well—just enough to say hello to him—but he had played football at my university before I was head coach. I knew who he was, and I knew this was a great loss, so I thought I would pay my respects as a head football coach and go to his funeral.

I'll never forget the day I walked into that church. The congregation was nearly 100 percent black. The church was full, and the only seat I could find was way up in the front, in the very first pew. I was aware that a lot of the people there would know who I was, and I tried to be inconspicuous as I walked to the front.

The service didn't start right away—there was just some music playing. But as I listened to it, I began to choke up. I couldn't help myself—I got tears in my eyes. I didn't want anyone to notice me, but there was such pain in that music; there was such sorrow in that music that it was breaking my heart, and I was unprepared for that. Then when the service started and people started to speak, I just lost it.

It was very odd, because people close to the family knew that I didn't know him well, but here I was, carrying on. I was doing everything that I could to keep my emotions under control, but it wasn't working. I was just sobbing, weeping, sniffling, and worrying that the family was thinking I was making a grandstand show of some kind. The entire service simply broke my heart.

I walked out of the church and knew that I needed to get in touch with that pain. I had been coaching black kids for years, and have been in their homes all across the country. I had been in ghettos. I had seen the circumstances and sometimes the depravity that these young, great athletes come out of. But I never understood the pain they were in. So I started to read, and I started to ask black guys I knew to explain things to me. It was very difficult for them. As I read, and as some of them opened up to me, I began to come in touch with oppression—real racial oppression.

The Beginning of Promise Keepers

A colleague and I invited 70 other guys to fast and pray about this. Interestingly, we invited only white guys. That's who we knew. I don't think there was a single black person there that day when 72 of us gathered to fast and pray to see what God wanted to do in the hearts of men across this nation. That was the beginning of Promise Keepers.

The following year there were 4200 men in the basketball arena in Boulder, Colorado. I gave my testimony, and we had a long program. It was a supercharged event, beyond anything any of us had ever experienced. Then it was time for me to close out the event. All I was going to do was get up and say that if each guy would bring 12 others, we could fill the football stadium next year. I was going to say, "Your responsibility is to bring 12 guys. You've got 12 months."

But just before I got up to the podium, I felt the spirit of God caution me and say, "Wait a minute. Look at the panorama of people here. What do you see?"

"I see guys who love Jesus," I said.

"What else do you see?" the Spirit asked.

Finally I got it.

"I see all white guys," I said.

The Lord spoke to me and said, "You can have 50,000 here next year, but if you don't have a full representation, I'm not coming."

So that's what I told the group. It didn't seem consistent with the Scripture verse that says, "Where two or three are gathered in my name, I am there," and people challenged my words, but I simply spoke what God had put in my heart.

The next year I started going outside the state of Colorado to talk to men about what God had put in my heart. But I'm not a preacher; I'm a reacher. I'm a guy who has a passion for the gospel of Jesus Christ, but I'm not given the kind of revelation that preachers have. So the only way I can get up to speak is if I go into a prayer room and close the door and go after God's heart. I just beg Him to tell me what's on His heart. As I would do that, I would write it down.

The message He gave me made me weep. My response was much more out of control than it had been at that funeral at the church in Denver. I just wept over and over as I wrote the message about the damage of the oppression born out of our country's racial hatred.

"Just Be Obedient"

I went to five cities: Dallas, Indianapolis, Denver, Anaheim, and Portland. At Indianapolis there were 1500 men packed in the church. When I walked in and sat down, a 60-year-old guy stood up and screamed with such a piercing, heartfelt statement, "It's the greatest day of my life, Coach!" When they introduced me, there was so much excitement in the room that they gave me a five-minute standing ovation. It was unbelievable.

Then when I spoke the message that God had put in my heart, it was like a pin in the bubble. It burst everybody's excitement. When I was done, the room just sat there, sober.

I got several letters saying, "What right do you have to come and talk to us about these things? You weren't advertised to come and say things like this. I traveled 200 miles to hear what you had to say about Promise Keepers, and instead you gave us *that*. What a disappointment."

I went back to my prayer room and I thought, "Lord, where did I miss it?" But the answer I got was, "Just be obedient."

So I continued to travel to other cities and speak that message God had given me. Anaheim had the same negative reaction. So did Dallas, where I felt tremendous oppression in a black church where half the guys were black.

Then I went to Portland, Oregon. When I got into town, the guys who picked me up at the airport said that they had just had a Billy Graham crusade there, the greatest of all time, they said, and they wanted me to know that there was no problem in Portland with blacks and whites—it's all been solved, they said. I took them at their word, but still felt that God had given me a message to deliver to them.

Inside the church was the same feeling as had been in Indianapolis. There was an electric, supercharged atmosphere there. And when I spoke, the same thing happened. I stole their thunder. They just sat there, looking at me when I finished. I knew then that, regardless of what the guys told me at the airport, things weren't any different in Portland from anywhere else. Then a guy walked up to the podium. It was unorchestrated, unannounced. He was a very distinguished-looking black man in his 60s, a preacher, and he stood at the podium. He was a guy whom everyone knew, and he had the respect of the people in the room.

For the longest time, he stood at the podium, tears coming down his cheeks. Finally, he said, "I never thought in my lifetime that I would hear from a white man what this guy said." Then he said these four words, which made my spirit resonate in a way that it hadn't for months. "Maybe there is hope."

When he said that, the Spirit of God just grabbed me by the heart and said, "You are speaking exactly what I asked you to speak. You have heard from Me." Ever since that moment, I have known a greater portion of what God is doing.

When John the Baptist heralded the first coming of Christ, he called men to repentance, and Scripture tells us that those who heard the message were convicted and were sorrowful for their sins and had a new determination to live a holy life. That response is similar to what occurred with Promise Keepers. Wherever we went, there was true sorrow for sin and a new hunger in the hearts of men for holiness.

But remember what John the Baptist said to those guys: "Produce fruit in keeping with your repentance."

"What should we do then?" they asked.

And John the Baptist told them what righteousness looked like. "The man with two tunics should share with him who has none, and the one who has food should do the same."

In Micah 6:8, Scripture says, "He has showed you, O man, what is good. And what does the LORD require of you? To act justly and to love mercy and to walk humbly with your God."

Three Questions

Doing justice means seeing the need in others and responding to it. So, in that context, for years I asked God three questions every day. These questions were foremost on my heart. They still are part of who I am. It didn't matter when I woke up—even if it was in the middle of the night. God's Spirit came to me with these three questions:

1. Lord, what is Your strategy to end racism?

2. What is Your direction for Promise Keepers? Where would You have it go? Is it going all over the world? What is it intended to do? What is it supposed to look like?

3. Lord, if I get an opportunity to speak, what would You have me say? What is on Your heart?

I believe God gave me the answers to these questions. I also believe the answer is going to disappoint you. The answer is the most underestimated activity in the church. It's the most misunderstood, overlooked, and neglected area of the church.

Almighty God is going to respond through prayer.

In Matthew 18:18, Jesus said, "Whatever you bind on earth will be bound in heaven, and whatever you loose on earth will be loosed in heaven." Heaven waits for earth to ask Almighty God to do what He wants to do. God has a perfect, holy, righteous will, and His will is set, but there's a problem. He has given man a free will. Every single person has a free will, and God will not mandate His will on man. If He did, we wouldn't have a free will. So what God is waiting for is for man to ask Him to do what He already wants to do. I believe with all my heart that God has a backlog of things that He is waiting on, but they won't happen until we pray and ask God to do what He wants to do.

Jesus then says, "Again, I tell you that if two of you on earth agree about anything you ask for, it will be done for you by my Father in heaven. For where two or three come together in my name, there am I with them" (Matthew 18:19,20).

The problem is that we have misunderstood this verse. It means that when two are gathered by the Lord in harmony, in the same spirit, stripped, barren, coming before the Lord with no agenda, no suspicions, no judgment, no unforgiveness in their hearts, no condemnation, when we come before the Lord that way, that's when Jesus will come, because that's when He can have His way.

When we come before the Lord and say, "Lord, all my hope is in You. My opinions don't count. I surrender my attitudes to You. You alone are supreme. You alone have the right to evaluate another man's life and behavior," it's in that context that Almighty God will move. And what God is waiting for is for the church to stand together and ask Him to do what He already wants to do.

This is the concept that changed my life. Some people won't understand this because they just won't let go of their opinions. They're saying, "No, I have a right to think what I want to think about that person over there, because that guy betrayed me, and I'm going to hold onto that."

We look around and see the obvious inadequacies and discrepancies in people around us, and we refuse to acknowledge the fact that we don't have a right to the suspicions and opinions we have. But if you're willing to have a clean slate, this concept can change your life, too.

The spirit of prayer is when we pray God's will back to Him. The spirit of prayer is when we echo the very heart of God right back to Him. That's when you have a spirit of prayer on you. When that happens, the only thing that matters to you is, "God, tell me Your will, and I will repeat it back to You. That's my highest calling in life."

Matthew 6:6 says, "When you pray, go into your room, close the door and pray to your Father, who is unseen. Then your Father, who sees what is done in secret, will reward you."

Have you ever thought about what that reward is? Do you know what God desires to give us? It's much better than answered prayer. God knows what we need before we ask for it. So when we talk about answered prayer, the reward isn't simply the things we're asking for. It's so much bigger. Every time we secretly go to God in prayer, where we shut everybody and everything else out, He gives us a greater portion of His heart. We actually inch closer to the very heart of God. We take it up a degree—maybe to the boiling point. We move into a relationship where nothing that we have in our human experience is anything compared to this. This is life's real quest. If we will go after Him, He will give us everything that is in His heart. As the mountains surround Jerusalem, so the heart of God will surround those who are after His heart. He will give us His wisdom, knowledge, understanding, the fear and power of the Lord. Those are the gifts. That's the reward.

What does this prayer look like? It's strenuous. It's work. But James 5:16 says, "The prayer of a righteous man is powerful and effective." When you know God's will, you can be fervent. When you're praying back to Him what you already know He wants to do, that's real warfare against the enemy. Prayer is red-hot. Prayer is full of fire. Prayer is from the heart. When it melts down from the head to the heart, that's what makes a prayer warrior.

The Greatest Competitor

As a coach, I've been around a lot of great competitors. I spoke at one of the Dallas Cowboys' chapels, and there were imposing guys sitting in that room. Emmitt Smith was there. I just looked at him, because he is such an incredible competitor, and I said, "I've been around a lot of great competitors, and there are great competitors in this room, but the greatest competitors of all are prayer warriors. A prayer warrior is totally selfless. A prayer warrior has abandoned himself. God says that He will not reject a broken and contrite heart. I've seen a lot of guys who can labor hard on a Saturday afternoon football field or a basketball arena, but the person who labors before God's heart, only wanting His will, interceding for others, that's a real competitor. That's God's competitor. That's the one whose life is moving in the right direction. That's a person in touch with the purpose of his life."

At one of our Promise Keepers' conferences we had all of the pastors come forward, and we were going to close out the program, when one of the speakers got up and said, "I want to speak on behalf of the pastors to all the men here. We repent, because the average pastor in the United States prays three minutes a day. No wonder we don't have praying churches. We don't have praying pastors."

I believe that God, across the world, is speaking to us, calling to us, saying, "I want guys who are after My heart. I want guys who are focused on Me and My kingdom and My will. Who will stand up and be counted? Whose hearts are broken for Me?"

Here's a story of someone who knew God's heart. Paul and Silas had just been stripped and beaten. They were in pain, covered with blood. Their feet were in stocks. They were feverish and suffering.

> About midnight Paul and Silas were praying and singing hymns to God, and the other prisoners were listening to them. Suddenly there was such a violent earthquake that the foundations of the prison were shaken. At once all the prison doors flew open, and everybody's chains came loose. The jailer woke up, and when he saw the prison doors open, he drew his sword and was about to kill himself because he thought the prisoners had escaped. But Paul shouted, "Don't harm yourself! We are all here!" (Acts 16:25-28).

Why did Paul do that? Freedom was available, ready for him to take. He was able to get out from all of that suffering and oppression. Why did he do that? Because Paul knew

God's heart. He knew God's will. He knew that God wanted to save that prison guard and his family and some of the prisoners. And because he knew the will and the heart of God, he set his own need to escape on the back burner.

That's what this life of significance looks like. It's a tough call, but it's the only one that give us full direction and meaning and purpose in our lives.

We serve a great God. We serve a God we can't fathom. We can't dream up a prayer request that He can't meet. And today in this time of great strife, God is after guys who want His heart. And we can all have His heart. It is right there for us. All we have to do is go after it.

I met Jim Amos several years ago when a mutual friend suggested I call on him and welcome him to San Diego, where he had just assumed the presidency of Mail Boxes, Etc. (MBE). It turned out that Jim and I had several common friends from the years that he spent in the Washington D.C. area, where he was involved with the U.S. Chamber of Commerce and a consultant training company. Jim has had extensive experience in the franchising business, which is why he was brought in to run Mail Boxes, Etc., the largest nonfood franchise company in the world.

During our visit, Jim told me about his military experience with the Marine Corps, and specifically his experience of two different duty assignments in Vietnam. He then went over to his bookshelf and pulled out a book titled *The Memorial*. It was a book he wrote trying to tell the Vietnam experience as realistically as possible. Jim's tours in Vietnam culminated with his receiving 12 decorations, including the Purple Heart and the Cross of Gallantry. *The Memorial* was chosen by the American Library Association as one of the best books of 1990.

Jim's second book is titled *Focus or Failure: America at the Crossroads*. He was in the process of writing this book when I met him. As he shared his concept with me, I started to understand his heart which, for a macho, gung ho Marine, had great softness to it. He was also working on an after-school project to help inner-city kids. He felt that if a corporation could be put together for a variety of children's initiatives, the hearts of America could be changed one child at a time.

It was with this intent that Jim asked me to help form "MBE Foundation for Children's Initiatives." In September of 1998, a 501c.3 corporation was started, and we began telling the Foundation story to the 4000 MBE franchises in 60 countries. The idea was that they could help by putting a small plastic box on each of their counters, encouraging customers to support Children's Initiatives by putting coins into the box.

Jim and his wife, Micki, have two married daughters and reside in San Diego. They have continued to travel a great deal because of the nature of the business, and in particular because MBE would like to be in every population center in the free world. Jim continues to stay committed to his Lord, his family, and his community. *Semper Fi!*

8

The Character of the Leader

James H. Amos, Jr.

MOUNTAIN CLIMBERS USE PIECES OF EQUIPMENT called pitons to help them scale peaks. These pitons are spikes fitted at one end with an eye for securing a rope. The spikes get driven into the granite or ice, so that the climbers can put their weight on them and continue to ascend. Climbers trust these pitons with their lives.

In our day, in a world that can't seem to count on much of anything, there is a need for pitons we can hold onto. Life is a struggle, and we are all at times desperate for something that will hold us, something we can use to ascend to the next level. Sometimes we simply need pitons to keep us from falling. While there are many potential pitons to grasp, some are of more consequence than others.

I can think of at least three.

The first piton is commitment. A few years ago as part of the strategic planning process at Mail Boxes, Etc., our leadership council developed a statement of core values. One of the values we agreed on was "commitment," and it subsequently went on the walls of offices, cubicles, and hopefully into the hearts of those that serve the MBE brand.

Yet today, commitment seems pretty cheap. If the value of something is determined by the way it's treated, then commitment doesn't have much merit. It is cheap in marriage, cheap in business, cheap in politics, and cheap in athletics. We live in a time where we appear to be wrapped in cynicism, stuffed with unbelief, and rolled in doubt and fear. We have lost our way and appear to have blurred the concept of commitment.

When was the last time you remember anyone talking about "bridge-burning commitment"? I think this concept was lost in ancient history. When conquerors came into a new territory, they often burned the bridges they crossed, or at times their own ships to the waterline, saying, "This is it—there is no turning back." That reflects a kind of commitment that we need to consider anew today. To return to the mountain-climbing illustration, there is no possibility of backing down. The only direction to go is up. There are no other options.

I wonder what has happened to the meaning of that kind of commitment in relationships? I wonder where the vow "until death do us part" went? How important is the word *commitment?* As an example, for more than 200 years the motto of the United States Marine Corps has been *Semper Fidelis,* or "always faithful." I spent eight years in that organization, including two trips to Vietnam. Those words mean a great deal to me even today. So much so, that I often write them above my name when someone asks me to sign one of my books. *Semper Fidelis* reminds us that we should exemplify bridge-burning commitment in the crucial areas of our lives.

Being faithful and being committed isn't a function of personal convenience. I am well aware that I'm capable of lacking commitment when things get difficult. Yet, I know that commitment isn't a function of self-indulgence, happiness, or economics. It's a function of doing the right thing, even if the cost is dear. As such, commitment doesn't appear to reflect the reality of our culture anymore.

Commitment means sticking around until the finish. How many people set out to run the 95-yard dash, or the 215, or the 435? Not very many. If they run and want to win, they have to race to the end: the 100, 220, or 440. Moreover, the real lessons in life are often in those final yards or meters, because finishing the race usually involves more pain, suffering, and sacrifice than the losers are willing to make. I have had to learn those lessons the hard way, and I suspect so have many of you.

I remember lying on the jungle floor in Vietnam with my helmet over my head, believing I was going to die, when I was supposed to be leading. I remember making a decision to sink a business. I remember integrity failures. These defeats cause us to take an inward journey, where we reflect on things we're not proud of. This inward journey is the most difficult in life, because the answers there are not memorized. It means coming face-to-face with the reality of who and what we are. Embracing a piton like commitment and applying it to our lives is a challenge that requires almost superhuman effort, especially when the popular approach to pain, frustration, and sacrifice is to simply walk away.

"God, Let Me Feel Pain"

I read recently that someone with leprosy can lose nerve endings and ultimately break an arm or a leg or a finger without knowing it. Consequently, the prayer of a leper is, "God, let me feel pain." For them, pain is a gift from God. For me, it seems most of my life has been spent trying to avoid it. But is it not on the mountainside or in the valley where we renounce selfishness, renounce the desire to avoid difficulty, and embrace humility? This is where things most despised by the world often become our greatest teachers. These painful moments are the wake-up calls of our lives where we learn the real transition from follower to manager or leader. It is also where we learn what real strength is, and the true definition of success.

If we want a picture of what true commitment looks like, we only need to look at Jesus Christ who, as Philippians 2 tells us, followed His commitment to God all the way to the cross. Is that not the ultimate example of bridge-burning commitment? Of course, He had opportunities to say, "This is too hard, too painful, too stressful," but He didn't.

From the time He was tempted in the desert to the prayer He prayed in Gethsemane that God would remove this difficult task from Him, He was committed to trusting His relationship and purpose in His heavenly Father. I look at Christ's commitment, and then I look at my commitment to Christ, and I realize that I desire that kind of "don't look back" approach to faith. I want to keep looking forward, toward an eternal life in fellowship with God. Yet, I also recognize how easy it is to fall away from this type of commitment when things get difficult, painful, or stressful. I must look to the Lord as the example for bridge-burning commitments.

Today, instead of being encouraged to maintain our commitments to Christ or our spouses or our values, what we are taught is upside down and backward. When faced with a challenge, the dominant view is to cut and run. We're taught that the solution to pain, emptiness, or stress is found in an aspirin bottle, an adult beverage, entertainment, or in simply working harder. We don't want to be unduly stressed. We want to avoid pain. And, like the leper, we miss life's wake-up calls because we are not aware that we've broken a finger, an arm, or someone else's heart. We've lost our feelings. The nerve endings are gone, and we can no longer differentiate between joy and pain, wealth or poverty, good or bad, because we've missed the difference between truth and deceit. Christ took His commitment to the cross. We must do the same. In Exodus 1:12 is written, "The more they were oppressed, the more they multiplied and spread."

A Business's Highest Priority

Another piton is character. In Greek there's a word that means "to chisel," or to carve out in stone, to hammer out. That's where the word *character* comes from. It means taking an unpopular position. As an example, I don't believe the number-one purpose of a business is to make a profit. Some people get very exercised about this. Imagine having a publicly owned company, and you're in a room full of investment bankers as I was recently, and saying that profit isn't the company's top priority.

What I do believe is that the number-one purpose of business is to build character in others, to assist in raising people to a higher level of performance, excellence, and morals. Isn't that what Christ did with His disciples and with those He touched? Making money ought to be a by-product of building the character of men and women and rendering essential service to others. Profits come and go, but character is eternal. Developing Christlikeness in each other is more important than making money. If we do these things, it is my firm belief that the profit will take care of itself, not just in the short term or quantities, but in the long term as well.

I believe with all my heart that if we treat people right and attempt to do the right thing, and embrace the right values, reach for the right pitons, there will be plenty of profit for everyone. Maybe there won't be the exponential profits that are demanded in this society, but every need gets met, every service gets rendered, and most of all, hearts are changed. People are changed. There is a distinct possibility that the paradigm shift of this new century will have to do with this concept, that the ends do not justify the means, that means justifies the ends—that relationships mean far more than we thought.

Everyone has influence over other people every day. Changing lives and growing people should take precedence over making money. It's a cliché today to say that our number-one asset is people, but it's true. You've read the business reviews and the theoretical arguments about process and systems, substance, and fact. The reality is that people run systems, not the other way around. We should be growing people, teaching character, values, and attitudes by what we say and do at home, at work, and everywhere we go. Investing our lives in people brings the total return.

During Jesus' ministry on earth He addressed social systems that oppressed the poor, and He addressed the Pharisees' legalism, but mostly He addressed people and their need to be redeemed by God. When people are transformed, systems follow. When leaders focus on the people in their organizations and treat them the way Jesus would treat them, the bottom line takes care of itself.

The Importance of Words

The third piton has to do with words. I believe that our words are the most powerful instruments and influences in the world. Words are seeds that are planted in the heart for good or evil. They are capable of echoing down through eternity. We have the opportunity to stand on the precipice of eternity and yell out, "I hate you, I hate you," or, "I love you, I love you," and rest assured what we yell out will return full force. Words presage deeds, and deeds reveal character.

As Samuel Johnson said more than 200 years ago, "Words are the dress of our thoughts." They're containers filled with emotions and meaning and mental pictures of information. They are planted in hearts where they take root and grow.

Words can be used to show affirmation and respect. Or words can ridicule and insult, embarrass or demean, belittle or dishonor. Words can tear apart relationships and, ultimately, the very fabric of tradition and history. The character of men and women can be seen by the choice of their words, which are evidence of the respect, attitudes, and motives of their hearts. There is power in words to speak life or to speak death. What words should we speak?

The Gospel of John begins, "In the beginning was the Word, and the Word was with God, and the Word was God." The Word that John describes is Jesus Christ, and the Word that we speak to each other can be the same. In the way we talk to each other, we can be saying *Jesus* and reflecting Him in all that we say. How carefully do we choose our words? Do we speak Jesus, speak life, speak love to each other? I wonder what would happen if everything we said was filtered through *Coram Deus*, "in God's gaze"?

There is no requirement for an abundance of words in order to speak life and love. For example, just six words alone can be very powerful. How about, *I admit I made a mistake?* Tough to admit, but essential in life and relationships. Five words spoken, *You did a good job,* can be profound. It's amazing to me, as hard as we try to recognize people at Mail Boxes, Etc. and celebrate their success, it's clear people cannot get enough praise. The human spirit is desperate for affirmation.

Four little words like, *What is your opinion?* can make all the difference. You don't hear that asked very much today.

What are perhaps the three most important words we can speak? *I love you*. Our lives are defined by the people who choose to love us and by those who choose not to love us.

Two words of significance are *forgive me.* We can't pass through this life without needing a ton of forgiveness. Every relationship that endures, requires it.

The single most important word is *we.*

The least-important word is *I.*

In a recent e-mail I received from a disgruntled staff member, there were 37 *I*'s. That revealed a large part of this individual's problem. Yes, the words we speak are important, powerful representations of who and what we are.

These three pitons, commitment, character, and words, are ways in which we reveal our trust in Christ to the world. They enable us to assist in transforming hearts one person at a time. They offer support for the journey—the climb toward eternal life in Jesus Christ.

At the end of the day, it is men and women of genius that are admired. Men and women of wealth are envied. Men and women of power are feared. But men and women of character are trusted. This is what is at the top of the mountain that we are climbing: eternal life in Christ through faith and trust in His Word. Our character, commitment, and words are pitons that can be grasped to anchor and stabilize our way.

Chuck Buck is a legend in his industry. As a third-generation descendant of his company's founder, Chuck has not only followed in the footsteps of his grandfather and father, but he has taken the entire family and their business to a new level.

I first met Chuck at a local outreach function for business and professional leaders. He was confident about who he was and why he was there, but he also had a humility about him that was genuine.

He told our group of professionals the very moving account of the Buck knife story, along with the personal story of his family life—an account that he had only shared a few times outside his family.

That evening, just 12 hours after sharing his very personal and emotional story, his brand-new 10,000-square-foot home of less than six months burned to the ground. When I called Chuck, he told me that he and Lori felt a peace even watching the fire. They knew God had everything under control. He also mentioned that no one was hurt and that most of the things could be replaced. The peace that transcends all understanding was very evident to me as he spoke.

9

Mixing Faith with Business

Chuck Buck

OCCASIONALLY WE GET LETTERS LIKE THIS AT Buck Knives:

> Dear Mr. Buck,
>
> This is my first Buck knife, and you may be assured it will be my last. I detest religious evangelism, and I was very offended by the tract I found hidden in the box. I feel this sort of message has no place in what should be a strictly commercial transaction between buyer and seller. Ordinarily I would express my displeasure by promptly returning the knife to the store and selecting another brand. However, this was a gift and I must keep it to avoid hurt feelings of the giver; therefore this note is the ONLY protest immediately available to me. You may be certain that I will make a lifetime silent protest by never ever buying a Buck knife.

We have always put a gospel message in the packaging of our knives, telling customers that God loves them and that Jesus died for their sins. Letters like this raise a question worth asking: Is it a good idea to mix Christianity with business?

Some background on our company might be in order.

My granddad made the first Buck knife in 1902 in Leavenworth, Kansas—outside the prison walls, in case you're wondering! He found old, worn-out files while he was working as an apprentice blacksmith. The workers would file horses' hooves, and after a while would discard the files. So he collected them and made knives out of them. A steel file has enough carbon in it to become very hard if it's tempered properly. Grandpa Hoyt made a few knives and gave them to friends. They liked them, and they had friends who wanted knives, so they started collecting files for him. Pretty soon he began charging money for his knives.

After his father passed away, his family moved to the Pacific Northwest, where he met and married Daisy and raised a family. During this time, he also accepted Christ as his Savior. As a lumberjack he started many small Bible-study groups with his fellow workers.

After their grown children left home, Hoyt and Daisy moved to Mountain Home, Idaho. There he pastored a small Assembly of God church. When World War II broke out, there was a call to get weapons to U.S. servicemen, so he set up a small shop in the church basement using a forge and grinding mandrel to shape, temper, and grind out knives.

In 1945 he and Daisy moved to San Diego where he taught my father, Al Buck, the skill of crafting Buck knives. The two men advertised in hunting magazines with a tiny ad and produced and sold about five knives a day while my mother sewed the sheaths.

I got into the business early on, and the company incorporated in 1961. Two years later we had a major financial crisis, to the point where we didn't know if we would survive. We had a major cash-flow problem and were unable to meet our financial commitments. My father called a special board meeting and said, "Fellas, I don't know where we're going to go with this company. It's obvious that this is a matter of life and death, and the only one I know to turn to is the Lord." We had a five-member board, three of whom were Christians. We asked God to open the doors, to give us wisdom, to give us direction, and to help us know what to do.

That night, when my dad went to bed, he told me that he had the name of a man on his mind—a local man who owned three sporting goods stores. When he awoke, the man's name was still on his mind. So he called the man and told him what was happening. He told him that we had a good business, that we were selling to dealers, but that they take 30 to 60 days to pay, and that we didn't have any working capital. The orders are here, my dad said, but we have to buy more materials and pay our employees. The man said, "I like your knives, and I give them away as gifts. I serve on the board of a local bank, and I'd like to introduce you to the president."

We met with him, and he gave us some good advice and loaned us money on our receivables for short-term financing. He also recommended that we sell another issue of corporate stock for long-term growth, which we did.

We make hunting and fishing knives, pocketknives, bayonets, and nearly every other conceivable kind of knife. We also made some collectible knives with material taken from the Statue of Liberty when it was being refurbished.

The Making of a Knife

In managing our company down through the years, I have noticed parallels between some of our manufacturing processes and the process of living a Christian life.

All of our knives go through a hardening process to make them excellent, reliable knives that hold an edge for a long time. For example, if we took one of our blades, stamped it, ground it, and put an edge on it—an edge so sharp a man could shave with it—and used that knife to cut some cardboard boxes, we would find that the edge would dull very rapidly.

To avoid that, we harden the blade by putting it in our 60-foot-long tunnel furnace, where the blade is subjected to 2000° heat for 45 minutes as it travels through the furnace on a conveyer belt. This process causes something to happen inside that steel. The martensitic condition is challenged and the molecules align.

If the blade could think, it wouldn't know why this was happening or whether anyone was in charge. But our engineers know every detail of this process. They know the content of the blade, its entire anatomy. The blade might think, "I don't want to be here. This really hurts. I'm going through this furnace and it's very uncomfortable." When we finally take it out of the furnace, it might say, "Whew—I'm glad that's over!" But then we plunge it into a deep freeze at 300° below zero. It might not know why it's in there, and it probably wouldn't know that it was changing. But the engineers know that the steel is being stabilized and it's becoming a tougher blade.

Then we bring it back to room temperature, and next put it into a 450° tempering furnace. That makes the blade very tough, but not brittle. Now we have a Buck knife. Now it's ready for our name. Now it's ready for use in its master's service.

Have you gone through a process like that? I have. I have been through a fire and a freeze and then back into the fire. Sometimes I wondered if I would ever get out. At times I didn't want to get out alive. I prayed for God's help.

A Marriage Crisis

There are different events in a man's life that cause the furnace to begin its work. For me that event was unfaithfulness to my wife. I prayed and asked God to forgive me, but God seemed to be deaf to my cries. I knew I had done wrong, so I changed my behavior and counted on the Bible's promise that God would forgive me. I knew that the Bible said not only would God forgive me, but He would also pardon me, and that He would even forget it ever happened.

The problem was that I hadn't told my wife, Lori. I carried this secret in my heart for a year, and finally couldn't stand it any longer. I didn't want anything between us. One Sunday morning, I told her what I had done. My thinking was that it had been a year, I had behaved myself, and everything would be fine.

It didn't work out that way. The news destroyed her—wiped her out. She had ups and downs, anger, denial, and all the grief steps that people go through. I honestly didn't know if she would stay with me. But I felt led to just support her, take care of her, and let her make a decision about what to do. She had every reason to leave, since I had committed adultery. She thought about it, we spent a lot of time communicating, which is what we should have been doing all along, and then she decided she wanted to talk to her mom in Arkansas about it. Since she didn't get along with her stepdad, she asked me to go with her.

The airlines were on strike at the time, so we got in my little 1974 Corvette and drove. We stopped in Tulsa, and in the hotel room she started acting very strangely. She went stiff, in a catatonic state. She just stared at me, wouldn't speak, wouldn't move. I thought she had snapped mentally, so I called an ambulance, and they took her to the hospital. I wondered if I would ever see her again, or if she would ever be normal again. It was my time of being taken through the furnace. I prayed, but I didn't feel that God was listening. I was so depressed about my situation that I contemplated driving that Corvette over a cliff and ending it all. I felt that without Lori, life wasn't worth living. But all along, the Master Physician was in control.

In the middle of my discouragement and depression, the hospital called and said they wanted me to come to the hospital to pay the ambulance bill. I decided I would go to the hospital, pay the bill, sign the insurance papers, and then drive my car over the cliff. But when I got to the hospital, a nurse walked up the hall and asked if Mr. Buck was here.

She told me that my wife was asking for me. That sparked a tremendous hope in my heart.

When I walked into the emergency room, our eyes met and she smiled the warmest smile I had ever seen. That smile and the look in her eyes wiped me out. But we weren't out of the furnace yet.

The Power of the Cross

Lori has always had a strong faith in God and seeks Him diligently for direction. She decided to stay with me, and while I wish I could say that everything was fine immediately, I cannot. The next two years were awful. Obviously, she didn't know if she could trust me. If I was at a business meeting and was home later than I told her I would be, she got very concerned. I assured her that I wasn't cheating on her, and I knew that I had to earn back her trust. At times it didn't seem we were making much progress, but the Great Physician was still at work in our lives.

For Lori, it seemed everyone wanted her to live and act as though nothing had ever happened. It seemed to her that since she still felt pain, she hadn't fully forgiven me. This was an intense time of struggle for her.

One night while lying in bed, she said she felt absolutely overwhelmed with the responsibility she thought that other Christians were requiring of her in this situation. It was then that the Lord threw her a lifeline.

A picture began to form in her mind of all that Christ had accomplished for us on the cross. For her the emphasis had been forgiving me, but something else became very real to her that night. She saw in Christ's death on the cross a twofold meaning. One was that He died that we might have forgiveness for our sins, and the second was that through His stripes we are healed. The cross not only represented forgiveness, but healing.

In her mind, Lori saw the cross reflecting the love of God to us and shared through us to others. She pictured two broken hearts kneeling at the foot of the cross, one in need of forgiveness and the other in need of healing, for truly a broken heart needs the healing touch of the Master's hand. It became evident to her that she could be an instrument of sharing God's forgiveness for me and that I could be an instrument of God's healing through standing by her and allowing the hurt to heal in her.

First Peter 1:6,7 says, "In this you greatly rejoice, though now for a little while you may have had to suffer grief in all kinds of trials. These have come so that your faith—of greater worth than gold, which perishes even though refined by fire—may be proved genuine and may result in praise, glory and honor when Jesus Christ is revealed."

I had been through that fire, and then through freezing spiritual temperatures when it felt like God was a million miles away. Over the years I've found God to be faithful in extreme situations needing healing and forgiveness. Today, Lori and I are the best of friends and her hurt has been completely healed.

A Message of Hope

Lori and I were so thankful for what God had done in our lives and marriage that we approached my father about including a Christian message of hope in the 2½ million knives we ship out annually. He agreed and, as a result, we occasionally get letters like the one mentioned earlier.

But in answer to the question as to whether it's good practice to mix business with Christianity, here is another letter I received from a woman who had purchased a Buck knife:

> I was very discouraged and depressed. I had lost all of my relationships, and I decided to commit suicide. I was led to this knife at the store, this Buck knife. When I

> got home and pulled the knife from the box, a piece of paper fell out. I read your message that God loved me, and something stopped me from taking my life. I realized that God really did love me and I decided I didn't want to hurt myself anymore. I just had to write and tell you to keep putting the message in for people like me.

As CEO of the company, I want to make sure that everyone is satisfied. When I get letters like the one from the atheist who was offended by the gospel message in our package, I usually write back and tell the person I'm sorry to have offended him, but that my purpose was to share the good news that God loves us, and that I've found eternal life by accepting Jesus Christ as my Lord and Savior. But in one of the few times in my life that I felt God spoke specifically to me, I sensed Him saying, "The man who wrote that letter isn't angry with you. He's angry with Me."

I couldn't believe that God had taken the time to speak directly to me. He was telling me that I didn't have to defend the faith. I just had to share it and let people make up their own minds. It took a lot of pressure off. And it was fantastic to sense that God was using me as a way to advance His kingdom. But remember, I had been through the furnace, and now I was ready for His use.

One other letter serves as a reminder for how God uses those messages in the packaging:

> I was on a committee to solicit companies for products to be auctioned off at our benefit banquet. You were kind enough to send one of your knives. I have always wanted a Buck knife, so I decided not to turn it into the banquet, but to keep it for myself. While

> I was examining the knife, I noticed the small note about God that you put into the knife box. I read it, and felt conviction for what I planned to do. I'm a Christian, and I asked God to forgive me, and I turned the knife into the banquet. I just wanted to ask you if you would forgive me, also.

I'm a pretty strong guy, but that letter wiped me out. I got out another knife and sent it to him. It was a refined knife that had been through the fire, and was ready for use in the hands of God.

Ron Harris and I have been personal friends for nearly 30 years. We met soon after Ron became a Christian in 1971.

Ron was senior vice-president and cashier of the First National Bank of Denver during the 1970s and had many opportunities to share his faith with other people in the business community. He subsequently served as executive director of a Christian missionary organization, followed by serving as a senior executive of business enterprises in the Denver area. He retired in 1997 from active business involvement, but stays very active in the ministry of helping others.

Throughout his working and personal life, Ron has grown as a businessman, husband, and father. He and his wife, Maribeth, live in Colorado.

10

Intimacy

Ronald Harris

MOST BUSINESS BOOKS AND ARTICLES I'VE read talk about the importance of good relationships with customers, investors, and employees. Some corporate leaders talk about how their employees are their greatest resource. Managers are instructed on how they should act around their people. Some are told to wander around the workplace and be accessible, others are told to socialize with their employees, while yet others are told to maintain distance from the workers they supervise.

All of this sometimes contradictory advice is important at some level because it addresses the importance of relationships, and good relationships are crucial to success in business. But there's another relationship that's often ignored by businessmen, and yet it's the most significant one of all—and that's a relationship with Jesus Christ. And second only to that spiritual relationship with God is one that also is usually passed over by most books and articles on business success. In fact, it's the relationship that often gets the least amount of attention from businessmen, but has the highest priority in God's eyes—and that's the relationship a married businessman has with his wife. How a man relates to his wife will have a direct effect on his relationship with Christ and will also impact his business life.

One of the biggest surprises of my life came when, after I had been married for ten years, my wife said to me, "I'm out of here." I'm the first guy to admit that I didn't have good teaching or training going into my marriage. There were no good examples or role models in my family. No one ever talked to me about what was important in marriage. What I observed as a kid didn't serve me very well. My mother was a single parent at age 19. My older sister and I were a hardship on my mother. As I look back over the years of her life and see what she did to hold our family together, I think she is the most courageous woman I will ever know. Fortunately for us, her father provided a small amount of money to her on a regular basis so she could stay home and take care of my sister and me.

When I was eight, my mother married a man returning from World War II who also had an eight-year-old boy. My stepfather was manic-depressive, and in those days there wasn't much help for people in that condition. He did have shock treatments, but he was never really able to deal with this disability in his life. As a result, our family life was difficult. We never knew if he was going to be on such a high that everything was unreal, or if he would be so low as to not be speaking to us. From day to day, we never knew what to expect. By today's standards it would be called a dysfunctional family. But we survived it.

Form over Substance

I got married when I was 22, still at the age where I thought I knew it all. No one needed to teach me anything. We had children early in marriage, and I set out in the world to do what I thought I was supposed to do. My understanding was that life was about success, title, money, and power. Looking back, I was seeking form over substance. All of my emphasis was on how I could get ahead. Anyone who tried to speak to me about any of my problems wasn't worth listening to. Corrective action wasn't part of my formula.

So when my wife came to me after ten years of marriage and said she was leaving me, I said, "Hello, we have three children, we have a nice house, we have two cars, we have a dog, I'm vice president of a bank. What are you talking about?"

She said, "There's nothing going on between us. You've got your golf game and your job. You're a busy man. But we don't have a relationship." I didn't have a clue as to what she was talking about. I thought we had a great relationship. My friends thought we had a great relationship. When I told my friends that my wife wanted to end our marriage, they said, "What's the deal with her? You have a great marriage!"

As I look back, I know that what she was really telling me was that we didn't have an emotionally intimate relationship. But even if she had said those words then, I wouldn't have understood her. Her decision filled me with shock and despair. It was out of my control, beyond me.

The Bible says "Haven't you read...that at the beginning the Creator 'made them male and female,' and said, 'For this reason a man will leave his father and mother and be united to his wife, and the two will become one flesh'?" (Matthew 19:4,5). I understood the "one flesh" part. My idea of a relationship was on the physical plane. As long as we had a great sexual relationship, we had a great relationship, right? But so much more is in that verse than just references to sex.

An Issue of Control

When God says, "A man will leave his father and mother," He's also talking about leaving emotionally. I confess that I didn't do that. I left a lot of stuff connected. Everybody does that to a certain extent. In family structures we all play various roles. It could be scapegoat, favorite child, or something else. We try to leave those roles behind when we establish our own families, but most of us take those old roles with us.

We also take family commandments with us. "Cleanliness is next to godliness" was a family commandment in my home as I grew up. Laundry and housecleaning were done on Monday. My wife's mother told my daughter without equivocation that Mondays were for cleaning. Other life commandments have a lot to do with control. My mother, as a single parent, had been very controlling in my life. I grew up not wanting a woman to control me because of my mother's total influence on me as a boy. As an adult, my role became one of wanting to control everything—particularly women. It didn't take long for my son to pick up on that. When I would leave home, he would try to take over. I would go on a business trip, and he would step into that role. He was six at the time.

But part of leaving your father and mother to marry someone means that you're leaving behind that old relationship to form a brand-new one with another person. You're connecting in new ways with your spouse. It also means loving that person as much as you love yourself. It means being willing to die for that person. But I'm not just talking about physically dying for her, as in taking a bullet for her. There's no heroism in that. I'm talking about dying to who you are and being willing to become the person she needs you to be. That way of living for her is what dying for her really means. This is harder than physically dying. It's what we are instructed to do as men.

The Bible tells husbands:

> Love your wives, just as Christ loved the church and gave himself up for her to make her holy, cleansing her by the washing with water through the word, and to present her to himself as a radiant church, without stain or wrinkle or any other blemish, but holy and blameless. In this same way, husbands ought to love their wives as their own bodies. He who loves his wife loves himself (Ephesians 5:25-28).

The Bible also tells us that God knows our hearts. That's one of God's characteristics. He listens to us, forgives us, and ministers to and encourages us. John 14:26 says, "But the Counselor, the Holy Spirit, whom the Father will send in my name, will teach you all things and will remind you of everything I have said to you."

Look at the characteristics of Christ's love for the church, and then remember that we're commanded to love our wives as Christ loved the church. That means we must have plenty of patience, long-suffering, and mercy toward our wives.

Proverbs 20:5 says, "The purposes of a man's heart are deep waters, but a man of understanding draws them out." I am convicted by the fact that I cannot tell you that I have always known the purposes of my wife's heart. I have not been that man of understanding who could draw her out and have her feel free enough to share all that was on her heart. I wasn't mature enough, not enough of a real man to hear and understand her. I have also not been the kind of man who could fully share my heart with her. I kept my heart guarded for many years, and yet my wife had been saying, "Let's share our hearts with each other." I didn't know what she was talking about.

Listening with One Ear

As I look at the characteristics of men today, of husbands interacting with their wives, I don't think we are very good listeners. We listen with one ear, preoccupied. We also don't offer much validation, but instead offer solutions. I am very results-oriented. So when my wife would begin to tell me about something, I was thinking about the solution to the topic she was describing. But that's not what she wanted or needed at all. She just wanted to tell me something and get a sense from me that what she was saying had meaning. I couldn't do that. I had to jump right in there with a solution, cut her off, give her the answer to the problem as quickly as I could. I was impatient and selfish, and it was one of the things God convicted me about when I became a Christian.

As you can imagine, things were pretty tense in our marriage after she told me she wanted out. I got a lot of sympathy from my friends, which didn't really help. But I was in despair. I didn't want my marriage to end. I had three kids, ages 7, 8, and 9, and I loved my family to the extent that I could understand the meaning of love.

In my desperation, I sought out my former boss, a man 30 years older than I am, walked into his office and said, "Lee, would you tell me again about how you became a Christian, and what happened?" Three years earlier, Lee had been my boss at the bank. He had invited me to attend a Bible study with him. He also invited some other guys from the office. He wanted to meet one morning a week at a local restaurant to read and talk about the Bible. I didn't want to do it, but I did it because he was the boss. Remember, my goal in life was success, and I thought to myself, *If this pleases him, it may help me get where I want to be.*

So I went to the Bible study and we took turns leading it. It was a terrifying experience, because if you attended it, you had to lead it occasionally. I remember having to lead a discussion on something out of the book of John, and I read that chapter at least 20 times, never finding anything to talk about. I couldn't see a thing in there. The person who led the discussion also had to lead the prayer before breakfast, so I took my Episcopal prayer book and held it low under the table and read from it, pretending it was really me praying. I did this for a year, just to get ahead, just to not be the guy who wouldn't go to the Bible study with the boss.

"Guess What Happened to Me?"

So now, three years later, my marriage was falling apart, and I was a mess. I sought out Lee and he shared his testimony again. He told about the problems he had had in his relationship with his wife. She had become a Christian and grew more interested in a relationship with her Christian friends than with him, and this caused him great concern. One night a bunch of her church friends were at the house, and she was in the kitchen with the women, while he was in the living room with the men. One of the guys said, "Lee, you look kind of down in the dumps." He said, "Yeah, I guess I need you guys to pray for me." They prayed for him, and he committed his life to Christ. That brief description was his testimony. I had heard his story earlier at one of those Bible studies, but at the time I thought to myself, *That's cool—he's an older guy and needs that stuff.* But every week when that Bible study ended, I was glad it was over and I was out of there.

Now I wanted to hear it again. He told it to me in 25 words or less, and then he prayed. He didn't pray specifically for me and my salvation, but he prayed.

I drove home in my little Mustang convertible, and as I was passing the Denver Country Club I said, "Jesus, time-out here. If You're who Lee says You are in his life, then I need You in my life. I need Your forgiveness. I need to confess to You that my whole life has been going in the opposite direction from where You want me to go."

Immediately I felt Jesus' presence in that car. It was real. Here I was, a guy whose personal life was in a shambles, and suddenly God was present in the car, giving me assurance of the future and forgiveness for the past, and I knew it. One of the first things He convicted me of was my selfishness, that my priority had been my career, my title, making money, concern for what others thought of me, my golf handicap.

I loved my wife and my kids, but God convicted me that they were more objects for my pleasure than anything else. So I drove home and said to my wife, Maribeth, "Guess what happened to me?"

I told her everything, and she said, "Whoa—another ploy." She thought that I was trying to convince her that things were going to be good. But for the first time in my life, I wanted Christ to be the center of our family. At dinner that night I shared it all with the kids. They were pretty young, and they said, "Yeah, whatever," and wandered off. But Maribeth and I talked until one in the morning. And God blessed that.

A few weeks later Lee dropped a brochure on my desk, announcing that a man named Larry Christenson, author of a book called *The Christian Family,* was coming to a church in Denver. I had only been a Christian for a few weeks and felt that I had a huge deficit in my life that needed to be filled, so I wanted to be wherever Christian people were. I went to the service and was surrounded by the singing, praising, and worshiping—something I had never experienced before. At the end of the service, I didn't want to leave.

Larry Christenson spoke from James 5:14,15, which says, "Is any one of you sick? He should call the elders of the church to pray over him and anoint him with oil in the name of the Lord. And the prayer offered in faith will make the sick person well; the Lord will raise him up." That sounded good to me. My daughter, Andy, suffered from epileptic seizures. It was severe, and she took a lot of medication for it. I talked with Larry Christenson about her, and he said that I could bring her over, and that he would pray for her. So I went home and told Andy about it, and asked her, "Do you believe Jesus heals people?" She said, "Yes." I nearly fainted. My wife had taken her to Roman Catholic catechism, and she told me she had heard that Jesus healed the lepers.

By gosh, she's right, I thought. So I told her, "I know a man who prays for people. Would you like to have him pray for you that Jesus would heal you of your seizures?"

So on Monday, during her lunch hour, I picked up my little seven-year-old girl from school. Larry talked with her briefly about Jesus being a light in her life, anointed her with oil, prayed for her, and we left.

I took her back to school, I went back to work, she quit taking her pills, and God healed her of the seizures. My wife couldn't believe it. I could believe it because I didn't know any better. I was a brand-new customer. Larry had said, "This is it," I said, "Let's do it," and I never had any struggle or confusion with it. But my wife said, "What's the deal here? What are you doing to our children? You become this whacked-out Christian guy, and now you're doing all this wild stuff to our children."

But even while she was hammering me about these things, God gave me the grace not to be defensive. She began to see that this truly was a change in my life. And Andy said to her, "Mom, I don't need to take the pills anymore. Jesus healed me." Maribeth also saw the books I had been leaving around the house, so she read some of them, and by the end of the year she committed her life to Christ. Our marriage survived.

Valuable Lessons

Some valuable lessons emerged over the years as our marriage grew stronger. I firmly believe that the marriage relationship is what God intends for us as His children. But that marriage relationship can produce healthy families and unhealthy families. I think a lot of the reasons there have been problems in families over the past generations up through the present is that husbands haven't taken the time to connect with their wives on a heart level the way the Bible tells us we should. If Christ died for us and now listens, counsels, intercedes for us, and if we are to love our wives as Christ loved us, then we should be doing the things at home that Christ did. God draws out the hearts of people. So should we.

All of us can look back at our family history and claim some level of dysfunction. There's nothing wrong with understanding what was going on back then. What *is* wrong is when we stay there. It's only reasonable to go back and say that something happened, or that I developed this way for these reasons. The thing to remember is that most of the time no one intended those things to happen. In many respects, our parents and their parents didn't know any better.

People who are still hampered by their upbringing may need help from a counselor, and they shouldn't hesitate to seek help. Nothing should hold us back. But it's also true that no one is so old that he can't change some things about himself. I had some pretty good excuses for why I was such a terrible husband and father. I also knew I needed to make some changes in my life, and I discovered that Jesus wanted to be in the middle of it all. The kind of change I am talking about didn't happen overnight. It was a long process.

From my experience and my observation of other relationships, I think the lessons I learned can apply to most marriages. We need to be better communicators. We need to listen, to make eye contact, to hear our wives when they speak, to give feedback, to ask a good question. I don't think many Christian people know how to communicate very well. We ought to be the people others want to talk to. They ought to know that they have our attention. I find that most Christians can't even ask a good question in a dinner conversation.

There's a good chance our wives already have books around the house on how to have a stronger marriage. We should read them. We also need to have people we are accountable to. We need to have people in our lives who will ask how we're doing in our relationships with our wives, and who won't accept a simple answer like, "Oh, great." We need people who won't be satisfied with surface answers, and who can point out our unhealthy habits.

Here's a suggestion that really goes out on a limb: If we're really committed to connecting at a heart level with our wives, we should say we want to forgo any sexual activity for 90 days, and that we want to focus on achieving a connected, communicating relationship instead. If our wives know that we're sincere, and that all we want is to learn how to connect in a way we have never connected before, premarriage or postmarriage, it will do wonders.

At the end of those 90 days, the sexual relationship will be better than anything anyone dreamed of. A lot of men think that if they just learn more techniques about sex, their sex lives will improve. That's not the answer. If you learn to connect with your wife on an emotionally intimate basis, everything about your marriage will improve.

Two Connected Relationships

Why is it important to connect at a heart level with our wives? Because by doing so we take a giant step toward connecting with the Lord. Trying to connect on an intimate level with the Lord while not connecting on an intimate level with our wives is almost impossible. The two relationships are connected to one another. Listening to our wives share their hearts, growing in that relationship, propels us into a more intimate relationship with the Lord. And if men think their wives are hateful, angry, critical, or just plain hard to please, it may be that they're frustrated because they have yet to experience an intimate relationship with men who are honestly striving to be the image of Christ.

Intimacy with our wives leads to intimacy with God. But we lack training in the area of intimacy. We have a lot of pride that gets in the way. Our upbringing gets in the way. But this is what God desires of us. He tells us in Ephesians

5 that the model for our relationship with Him is our relationship in our home.

When Jesus says in Matthew 25:41, "Depart from me, you who are cursed," some translations add, "I never knew you." I have thought about that phrase a lot, and I don't like the sound of it. In effect, Jesus is saying that we didn't have a heart-to-heart relationship. We didn't connect at that deep level. Jesus is saying, "you did things in My name, you used things in My name, but I never knew you." It's very similar to what my wife told me at the end of ten years of marriage. Her telling me she was leaving was another version of "I never knew you." We had a house, kids, and a sexual relationship, but we didn't know one another. We didn't connect at that deep, heart-sharing level. God saved that marriage. He saved Maribeth and me. And by drawing us into a closer relationship with each other, He drew us into a closer relationship with Him. If He can do it for us, He can do it for you.

Dick Capen is a man of many talents. In his busy career he's served as a director and senior executive at Knight-Ridder, Inc., during which time he spent seven years as publisher of the *Miami Herald.* He also served as deputy assistant secretary of defense and assistant to the secretary for legislative affairs. In 1992-93 he served as United States ambassador to Spain. He's the author of *Finish Strong: Living the Values That Take You the Distance,* published by HarperCollins. He has also served as a board member of the Billy Graham Evangelistic Association and presently is the director of Carnival Corporation and the American Funds.

Dick lives with his wife, Joan, in southern California.

11

Living Out Your Values

Dick Capen

WHEN I WAS PUBLISHER OF THE *MIAMI HERALD*, I lived in a community with a dynamic diversity of Jews, Catholics, and Protestants. Fifty-two percent of the population was Hispanic, 20 percent was black, and the rest was Anglo, like me. I was a minority. The *Miami Herald* has incredible influence in the entire state of Florida, and I worked very hard to maintain the paper's respect for the multiple races and religions our region represented. And while it is important to respect the views of other people, we also have a responsibility to stand up for what we believe.

At the beginning of my nine years as publisher of the *Herald*, I wanted to be a visible manager throughout the newspaper and the community. So I worked in the pressroom. I delivered newspapers. I sold advertising. I tried to get all around the operation of 3000 employees, nine editions a day, including one that went to 41 cities in South America. I got to know the diversity of the city, of the market, of our customers, and of our own employee base. Throughout this experience I felt that it was my responsibility, while respecting everyone else's rights, to be clear about who I was and to live out what I believed.

Almost every Sunday I wrote a column. It was essential that I be sensitive to our newspaper's diversity which, on Sundays, included more than a million readers. I suspect that many came to sense that my religious faith was important to me, but I tried never to carry it on my sleeve. In my opinion, the ultimate missionary work we have is in the ways we set an example.

In south Florida I had many close Jewish friends. I have a respect for their culture, their history, and their struggle for independence, reflected in the state of Israel. I always sought to learn and respect their point of view. I went to Israel for a week with the Jewish leadership of Florida and saw that nation from their perspective. But my friends also saw my wife and me read from the Sermon on the Mount, and they participated in a service with us at the Garden of Gethsemane. It was a wonderful experience. They shared their Jewish traditions and faith with us, and we had a chance to share ours with them. The trip was a very moving experience for each of us.

Living out our faith can be enriched, in my opinion, by using three principles.

The first is the principle of helping each other. Ephesians 2:10 says, "For we are God's workmanship, created in Christ Jesus to do good works, which God prepared in advance for us to do." When we help each other, we're showing the world what kind of people we are by putting actions to our faith.

A second principle comes out of Romans and has the theme of using our abilities well and realizing that there will be opportunities to change and to find new ways in which we can put abilities to work. Romans 12:6-9 says,

---

> We have different gifts, according to the grace given us. If a man's gift is prophesying, let him use it in proportion to his faith. If it is serving, let him serve; if it is teaching, let him teach; if it is encouraging, let him encourage; if it is contributing to the

needs of others, let him give generously; if it is leadership, let him govern diligently; if it is showing mercy, let him do it cheerfully. Love must be sincere.

This is a very commonly quoted chapter, and it's very true. God has given each of us the ability to do certain things well. I think it's also important to set an example for other people. Above all, my wife and I aspired to represent the best of America in all that we did while I served as U.S. ambassador to Spain. It was a whirlwind experience. We were literally driving across the country from Miami to San Diego, where we intended to live, when we got the call from President George Bush asking us to take that job. We reversed direction, put our belongings in storage, had to quickly brush up on our Spanish, get ready for the Senate confirmation hearings, prepare for the Olympics that were scheduled for Barcelona, and all the other things that were going on at that moment. Ninety days later we were in Madrid.

We had worked in government before, and as a result of that experience decided that it was critical to set priorities. It's so easy to get inundated by the work and the protocol and all the things that go with it. With the Olympics, the World's Fair, and the five hundredth anniversary celebration of Columbus's discovery, it really was the year of Spain when we were there.

Being Authentic

I decided that we were going to have three specific goals early on. One was to visit all 50 provinces in the first year, which we did. Another was to try to meet and encourage as many of our athletes as I could. This was the first time in history that there was a chapel in the Olympic Village. We went there one Sunday and prayed with an incredible group of former American Olympic athletes who traveled to Spain as volunteers to help our enormous American delegation.

Most of all, though, I decided that we were going to be who we were. We were going to live out our faith in authentic ways. The American embassy had a sizable staff and a large residence where we entertained 7000 people in one year. We decided that our life in Spain would reflect our values. To do this, we did a number of things that were apparently unusual. First, we invited the entire embassy staff over to the residence. That sounds like a common thing that any business person would do, but it had never been done before. But by having them in our home, we got to know the staff. We worked hard to be an encouragement to them. Many of the American families have problems living overseas, and those problems are not commonly known. They needed someone to care about them. As a further exercise of faith and to help meet these needs, my wife was asked to start a Bible study.

Also, in our family we have a tradition that when we pray at dinner, we always hold hands. That is not part of the Spanish tradition—men holding hands with women, much less men holding hands with men in prayer. It's not part of the Spanish tradition that women get up and speak in Spain. But Joan did, often starting our meal with a blessing in Spanish. That was our style, and I was proud of her for doing it.

Not everyone thought this was a great idea. A guest at one of our dinners was the editor of *El Tiempo,* which is the Spanish equivalent of our *Time* magazine. He took a cynical view of our practices and immediately told his colleagues about the arrogance of the ambassador, who was attempting to bring church and state together, simply because we said a little blessing before dinner. It became a feature story in *El Tiempo,* and I have it framed as a matter of pride.

During our tenure we visited dozens of Catholic cathedrals and basilicas throughout the country. At that time, we were the only diplomats who ever met all seven Spanish cardinals. There is a lot of antagonism between the church and state in Spain, but we tried to interact with everyone in a Christian way.

We also invited many of the Protestant missionaries in the country to our home. Until 1980 it had been illegal for them to function publicly, so they have been in a very lonely environment. When His Majesty Juan Carlos became king, he established a constitution that took powers away from his position and created the democracy that exists today. This allowed much more openness for diversity in religion. But until recently the missionaries' work hadn't been very effective. One person who had been there 20 years told me with great joy that during the past two decades he had seen 20 conversions to Christ. Talk about patience and humility!

The principles of helping others, using our abilities, setting an example, and living our values were important parts of our diplomatic service while I was ambassador. Through our work, I would like to think that Spaniards came to know something of what kind of people we are by the lives we led while in Spain.

The Power of Ethical Wills

There is another principle that I'm trying to apply to my life today. It has to do with setting the priorities of life. At a synagogue service in Miami, a rabbi spoke about an incredible story involving the Jewish ghetto in Warsaw, Poland, in the 1930s. At that time, there were approximately three million Jews in Poland. Parenthetically, there are fewer than 50,000 there today. By the late 1930s, thousands of Jews living in this ghetto were persecuted by the Nazis who began shutting the Jews' stores. Jews lost their bank accounts, their material resources, their homes, their furniture. They didn't know what was ahead, but it became clear that they were going to be relocated. As they lost their belongings, they began a process of preparing what are called "ethical wills." That is, they wrote down who they were. They wrote on a piece of paper the values that they felt were important to them. They were writing these wills to children and grandchildren yet unborn, to people they felt they might not ever see, but to whom they wanted to give the most important thing they had: their values. After writing these wills, they put them away in the basement of the synagogue, which was in the heart of the Jewish ghetto.

Miraculously, those "ethical wills" endured the tremendous bombing that took place when the Nazis invaded in the late 1930s, and again in 1945 when the Russians and Americans recaptured the city. The war virtually leveled Warsaw, including the ghetto, but somehow those wills survived. Some of them are now in the Holocaust Museum in Washington D.C., and some have been published in an anthology of ethical wills.

I was haunted by this story. As I left that service, I asked myself, "Who am I? What would happen if I knew I were to die tomorrow and I had the rest of the day to put down on paper the ultimate values that I wanted people to remember about me? Have I been living those values? Are they really the priority of my life? Does my wife think that those are my values? Would her list describing me match mine? What about my children? How will I be remembered by grandchildren, great-grandchildren, and other generations who will never know me in person, but can only know me by my legacy?"

What about you? If you knew you were going to die tomorrow, how would you be remembered? What are the most important things in your life? Is that the way your friends think of you? If not, what will you do to correct it?

Does your schedule today reflect your ultimate values? What about your schedule for the next five years?

What that rabbi described as he told me about these ethical wills struck me as a wonderful tradition. I've always believed that the best way to make a decision is to write the components of it on paper. The best way to get rid of anger is to put it down on paper, sleep on it overnight, and probably throw it away the next day when you see how foolish your thoughts were in the heat of the emotion.

Ethical wills are a wonderful way to transmit our values to future generations. Think of your own grandparents. Do you know if how you would describe them has any relationship to what they felt was important in their lives? Is that how you want to be judged by your grandchildren someday, or by others who will never have a chance to know you?

In an age of computers, videos, fax machines, CD-ROMS, and other technology, we have wonderful opportunities to establish in a very lasting way who we really are.

My Ethical Will

I was in the headline business for a long time, so I like to think of my ethical will as a collection of headlines that help set my course in life. Making such summaries may be useful to you. You can live them out daily, and you can then share them with your friends.

My challenge to you is to take this list and find Scripture verses that help confirm these values for your life and share them with your friends.

Feel free to adjust this list, or change the ranking and add new values that are important to you.

1. Take chances without fear of making mistakes.

2. Make choices and take charge of what you choose. (Maybe I've sparked something in your mind that you have been considering, and you're saying, "Well, I'll look at that

next month or next year. Maybe ten years from now the timing will be better." Timing is now.)

3. Be willing to change.

4. Don't torture yourself over the things you might have done. Chalk up your losses and move on.

5. When you embark on a new adventure, don't leave any of yourself on shore.

6. Earn the trust of other people. Everything starts with trust. If you can't trust the person who's running for president, if you can't trust your boss, if you can't trust your minister, if you can't trust your own spouse, if you can't trust your children, then who in the world can you trust?

There is a whole world of disillusioned, misled people who started out trusting their leaders and quickly lost that trust. They're very cynical, yet they're still looking for hope. If you lose a person's trust, it takes a long time to earn it back. Trust is built at home and at work with your colleagues. If you think you're such a great Christian and then you go to work and blow up at the office, or you treat someone in a disrespectful way, and that person knows that you brag about what a Christian you are, think of what a hypocrite you are in their eyes. You must trust each other and you must earn that trust every bit of the way. If you lose it, even in a small way, it takes a very long time to get it back.

7. Do your best, no matter how modest the task is. You never know who is watching, and in the end you must answer to the Lord for whatever you've done, including whether you gave a half-baked performance when you knew better.

8. Serve other people. We're going to have more cuts in the federal budget. It's going to be more important to serve other people, and it's a great American tradition. I was the head of the United Way in Miami. It was almost an impossible job because so many of the people there had come

from other cultures. Not many of them understood the concept of volunteerism. In South America, in the Caribbean, in Cuba, if there was a need, either the government filled it or nobody filled it. Volunteerism is a concept that we must constantly teach because, like everything else in our society, it's one generation away from extinction.

9. Be consistent in your beliefs. Don't try to be all things to all people. Be focused in everything you do.

10. Embrace diversity. So many of us in America live in a comfort zone, and in some respects we're more divided than ever. No one knows that better than I, living in Miami, where I spent a lot of time in the black community, the Haitian community, the Nicaraguan community, the Colombian community, and of course the Cuban community. I was the ultimate minority. I learned to speak Spanish. I went to synagogues and Catholic services and spoke there in English and Spanish.

Knight-Ridder had businesses in many countries, and I was amazed when I would go abroad how many of our business hosts know our language, understand our culture, and are informed on current events in America. Often I would travel overseas with very little preparation as to local customs and national affairs, and very limited ability to use another language. Sadly, too many Americans expect the rest of the world to adapt to us. There is a wonderful world of diversity out there, and we need to taste it.

11. Be an optimist. I believe that you can mix optimism with reality, but I want optimism by my side every step of the way. There are times when I couldn't possibly have survived without it, because it's all I had.

12. Set a moral compass in everything you do. Define your goals, set priorities, and stick with them. Above all, ask yourself as you develop priorities how you want to be remembered. What are your ultimate values? How can you

translate your faith into the real world where you have an opportunity to evangelize a huge number of people who need the inspiration that you can provide?

13. Finally, it is important to finish strong. After George Bush lost the presidential election in 1992, I wrote him a personal note to thank him for the inspiration he had provided to my family. He replied with a note that reminded me that we still had several weeks ahead on the job and that we should push ahead. "Finish strong," he said. I believe that statement profoundly. Whether you're 25 and finishing up in college, or you have a tough job to complete, you must finish strong.

And if you are well into the later years of life, you must finish strong. One of the great frustrations I have in coming back to southern California in retirement is to see people in their 40s and 50s who have retired mentally. They enjoy the incredible beauty of this area: the sun, the beach, the mountains, the desert, the golf, the tennis, the sailing, and whatever other trinkets they've picked up along the way, but they're brain-dead. They haven't grown at all. They have finished weak.

On the other hand, I've seen other people a lot older who are still going strong. Sherwood Wirt, the former editor of *Decision* magazine, is a good friend of mine, and he's almost 90. I was in a Bible study with him about 20 years ago, and he still meets with the group every other Friday. "Woody," as he's called, recently published his twenty-eighth book, this one on joy, and he did a lengthy and tiring book tour for it with his wife. I admire people like Woody who keep their minds active. Their bodies may be a little slow, but their minds are strong, and they're making valuable contributions to society. Regardless of a person's age, there is much he or she can do.

We have so many opportunities to live out our faith in our workplaces every day. My prayer is that we recognize those opportunities and use them to point people to Christ.

I first met Bob Buford at a Young President's Organization meeting where I heard him tell how he had decided to write his book *Halftime: Changing Your Game Plan from Success to Significance.* In that book I saw not only myself, but also many of my good friends who had achieved success but who were questioning their significance.

It's one thing to get a vision, think it through clearly, and then try to share it with others with such conviction that they see how it would apply to their lives. Bob had the ability to tell his message so succinctly that each of us could relate immediately. Both through hearing him speak and reading his book, I was able to see not only myself, but also many of my good friends and associates who were finishing the first half of life and heading into "halftime."

The question we face at such a time is, How do we separate the success portion of our life, whatever that means, from the portion of our life that spells out significance, whatever that means? We males seem to have a difficult time defining our lives with meaning and purpose.

It took a major tragedy in Bob's life to help him put definition to his dilemma. Bob has been able to take that tragedy and, together with his wife, Linda, they have rebuilt their family unit around each other with a love and determination that has been extremely encouraging to those of us that have been privileged enough to know them.

Until the sale of his company in July 1999, Bob served as chairman of the board and CEO of Buford Television, Inc., a family-owned business that started with a single ABC affiliate in Tyler, Texas, and grew to a network of cable systems across the country. In 1998, Bob launched FaithWorks, an organization that helps business and professional leaders convert their faith into action. Bob's also the author of *Game Plan: Winning Strategies for the Second Half of Your Life.* Bob and Linda make their home in Dallas, Texas.

12

Shaping the Second Half of Your Life

Bob Buford

IN THE FIRST HALF OF OUR LIVES, MANY OF US are focused on success-oriented issues. It's an intense period, where most of our energy goes. For me, it was a time of trying to raise my family and make my mark on the world. But inevitably there comes a period that I call halftime, where we wake up in midlife and say, "I wonder what I am going to do when I grow up!" It's a time of reassessment, of reevaluation. In the metaphor of a football game, it is where we come off the field for a little while and discuss what we did during the first half. But the most important part of halftime is deciding what we are going to do in the second half.

Believe me, most of us are coming off the field at a remarkable time in our lives. One hundred years ago, life expectancy for people in this country was around 50. Now, most people don't consider someone old until he is around 75 or more. It is a relatively new phenomenon that people live as long as they do. What this means is that we have been given an extra 25-30 years. For many, this second half will be a time of affluence, because kids are out of school, we've made and lost a lot of money, we have a lot of life experience, and the Rolodex of our lives is pretty substantial.

My life is probably pretty typical for people like me who are older than the baby boomers, but not retired. I was married at age 22, had a child a year later, and worked in my family business, which was operating television stations in small markets. It was a very exciting time for me. I think a lot of men enjoy a particular season in their lives where everything seems to be right.

In high school, I was pretty average. Then I went to college, and again was just average. But then I went into business and at last I was no longer average. It was my zone! Here was finally something I could grab onto, where I could set objectives, accomplish goals, and go after things. My life was in my own hands, and I was simply consumed by business.

After about ten years of this, I began to worry that I was so intense about business that I was going to lose the things that were important to me. This wasn't my halftime yet—maybe just a time-out. I had this feeling that I would be sucked up so far into business that I would find myself without a marriage and on the wrong side of raising my son. The question I began to ask was, "What am I going to lose with all of this gaining?" Another way to ask it is, "If my life worked out perfectly, what would be the things that I would want to retain, and how would they work?" What I was really looking for was balance. I wrote down some goals, and those framed the next ten years of my life.

Setting Goals

The first goal was to grow my business at a rate of ten percent per year. That's what I wrote down, anyway. The real goal I had was a ridiculous figure, so I put that one in the bottom left-hand drawer. I really wanted to run the company at 25 percent per year, but I didn't want to say that to anyone.

The second goal was to stay married to the same person I married in the first place.

The third was to raise my son to have high self-esteem. The fourth and fifth were that I wanted to grow culturally and intellectually. I didn't want to go brain-dead through this business and parenting activity!

If you compound anything at 25 percent per year, even if you've only started with $1.50, after several years you have some real money. That's what happened to our company. We were buying and selling television stations at a pace of one acquisition per year. As I look back, that period of life was my first half. It was intense, productive, and hard-charging. I was like a fighter pilot locked on target, and the plane wasn't going where the plane wanted to go but where the target went. Wherever that 25 percent goal was, that determined where I was to go.

As a result, I didn't really own my life. All of us at some time or another have given our lives over to some pursuit, and in a country like the United States, where you have so many choices, you can be tyrannized by those choices. It's an internal tyranny, where you surrender yourself to your goals and objectives. There were a lot of side effects that went along with my wanting to run my company at a very aggressive growth rate year after year. All of us can choose the game we want to play, but we can't choose the rules of the game. And if we give ourselves completely over to the game, as I did, we can become enslaved by it. And I was truly enslaved.

"Been There, Done That"

When I got into my mid 40s, I began to have this sense of "been there, done that." I had been in the warrior stage and felt great about it, had run my four-minute mile, and had gone where I wanted to go. It is the result, I think, of reaching your goal and having your goal release its hold on you. That tends to open you up. I had dodged a big bullet in my business, where a business I had sold lost several million dollars with its new owners, so I knew what it felt like to have a close call and to have a lot of success. But something inside me began to say, "There has got to be something God has in mind for me." It felt like a thaw or an opening up of my heart. This is what I call a person's half-time.

My internal dialogue moved me from wanting success to wanting significance. The problem was that, when I thought about what it meant to live a life of significance, I imagined it meant having to give up my life and be a full-time minister or something. It's wonderful that people are ministers, but it's also wonderful that I'm not one! The conclusion I came to was that what God wants from each of us is our availability. I think each of us will be held accountable for what we did with the person God made us to be.

I think there will be two questions on life's final exam. Maybe more, but I visualize it this way. The first will be, "What did you do about Jesus?" I can picture God saying, "I gave you friends, the Bible, 28 channels of religious television, skywriting over beaches. It was hard to miss Him. But what did you do about Him? Did you turn your back, or did you reach out and accept Him?" The second question will be, "What did you do with what I gave you to work with?" That's what the parable of the sower teaches us in Matthew 13.

Each of us had been given a unique temperament, a unique financial structure, a unique history of good and bad things. Some people have been abused as children, have suffered with alcoholism, have been through a traumatic divorce, have had a financial crisis, and those things are as much a part of our legacy as the good things in our lives. It's just part of our makeup. It is the whole inventory of our lives that God will hold us accountable for. He won't hold us accountable for what Campus Crusade did, or what Focus on the Family did, or anything anyone else did. He wants to know what we did with what we had to work with. That's the significance question. It's very personal.

God Uses People As He Has Built Them

When I experienced my own halftime, I learned five valuable lessons. The first was that, at halftime, I had to start with myself. I was frightened to death that if I ever gave my life completely over to God I would find myself as a missionary in some remote country. I knew that I would make a terrible missionary. I knew that I would be dead by the second day! I have talked to enough people to know that I am not alone in this kind of fear. So many of us are afraid that if we give ourselves to Christ, God is going to do something bizarre with us.

But in all of the halftime stories I have heard from countless people around the world, it doesn't happen that way at all. The way it works is that God uses people as He has built them—through their experience, through their lives, through their patterns of what made them who they are.

Peter Drucker, the management expert and social philosopher, has been a mentor to me in my second half. His emphasis has always been on building on our strengths. I firmly believe that, in the second half, building on the strength of the first half will make an enormous difference. To this day, I do not know how a television picture works. I can't do bookkeeping. Some people are very good at these things. What I know how to do is build a team, set and reach a goal, and implement a plan. When we give ourselves over to Christ, we still have to be good at what we're good at. The second half starts with us, with how we are made, with our strengths.

"What's in The Box for You?"

The second lesson I learned in my quest for significance was that I had to change the primary loyalty in my life. During this period of halftime, I made an appointment to see a management consultant I had worked with before.

He's a high-powered guy who charges 10,000 dollars per day, and had just worked with Coca-Cola on helping them get out of their fiasco of marketing the "New Coke." I was having trouble sorting things out, so I thought it was important to pay someone to help me think. Even though he is a committed atheist, he fires with more cylinders in his head than anyone else I know, and he's ruthless in how he goes for the center of things. He has an uncanny ability to cut to the core of an issue. My wife and I drove to Palm Springs to meet with him. I talked to him for a couple of hours about what was going on with me, and that I wanted a plan for me, not just for my company.

He said, "What I'm finding with companies, and really with individuals, is that people get their lives too complicated. They have too many things they are after—too many objectives. If you have 30 objectives, you have no objectives. The way I am doing planning now is asking people what's in the box." He took out a piece of paper and drew a box on it. "What's in the box for you? If it's Jesus Christ, or money, or whatever, I can tell you what the strategic planning implications are of that decision. But if you can't tell me what's in the box, you're going to waver between two values, the way I've seen you do for years, and as I've seen you do this morning, and you're going to be confused."

My wife, Linda, the consultant, and I were the only people in the room, and I think Linda and I saw our lives pass before our eyes. We were both thinking, "If we put *Jesus* in there, no more French meals, no more fun." But I wrote *Jesus* in that box.

Building off of the first rule, what God did was use me the way I am. I was an entrepreneur in my first half. Why did I think I wouldn't still be one in the second half? Peter Drucker says everyone should be able to put his life mission on a T-shirt. This is mine: "100X." It comes from the parable of the sower. I wanted to be the good soil that the seed fell into, where I would multiply it 100 times over.

That's what had happened with my business in the first half. I wanted to do it with lives in the second half.

The way that has happened is that the second half of my life has been focused on developing leadership networks for leadership teams of large churches. We are now serving at least 100 times more people than when we started. Being good soil is all about availability. Hard soil is unavailable. Rocky soil is superficial. I think that's where a lot of us are. The seed is the Word of God, and it gets planted, but it gets stunted by the care and concern of the world and by the pursuit of riches. Then the plant proves unfruitful. We're capable of being good soil that will produce 100 times the seed that was planted, but so often we end up just producing these pygmy plants.

God Can't Steer a Parked Car

Rule three is to work on this in parallel with the rest of your life. We're not leapers, so we shouldn't leap. We shouldn't burn our degrees, quit our day jobs, and just sit and try to start over. I think it's a good idea to keep our day jobs if God is working on us, because it allows us to put weight on each foot a little bit at a time. We can ease into becoming a board member, becoming a donor, and gradually shift our weight.

Over a period of about eight years, I was able to recapture about 80 percent of my time. We sold the family business and, while my brothers did something else with their time, I started this leadership program. The point is that it's okay to keep working for a while at what you have been doing, but it's important to get started in the new direction. Even God can't steer a parked car. We need to get in motion.

Maybe there is an aspect of your business that can be used in ministry. People who need help are within very close proximity to where you work. You don't have to proselytize them or convert them. You just need to help them.

Ask them how you can be useful to them. They'll figure out it's Jesus working and not you. They probably already know you wouldn't do this on your own. People are smart about these things.

The fourth rule is that this is hard, not easy. There isn't anything easy about getting a college degree. There isn't anything easy about learning a business. There isn't anything easy about staying well off. Life is not easy. Scott Peck in his book *The Road Less Traveled* sold millions of books saying life is hard, not easy. So why would people assume that if they were going to do some ministry kinds of things that it was going to be easy, and that all of the Christians are going to act like Christians? That's a puzzle to me. People will always act a little Christian and a little jerky, because that is how human beings are.

A businessman I know faced this very situation in Michigan. He sold his company and started a Christian organization in the education field that really addressed this significance issue. It was innovative, creative, and was going to make a big difference in people's lives. But about halfway into it, the company that had bought his firm said, "We are going to start a new division, and you have to run it for us. You're the only guy who can do it, and we'll build the organization around you, and..." Blah, blah, blah. Sure enough, he did it. When I saw him later I asked him why he did that, and he said, "It was just so easy. This Christian world, this education world, well, I don't know what I'm doing. I'm an amateur in those areas. I feel more secure with this company because it is familiar territory." I was disappointed, but what he said is true. The whole Christian world is different territory, and it's not made to accommodate people coming out of the work force.

There is a very smart man who heads a consulting firm in Manhattan who is a committed Christian, and he was facing this success and significance debate in his own life. He went to his Catholic priest and said he was sensing that he needed to be more available to God, that he wanted to do something that made a difference in people's lives, and that his work with his company was not doing that for him. So he asked his priest if the church could use him in some way. He said the priest just looked at him as if to say, "How in the world could I use you? You don't preach, you haven't been to seminary, you are not into chastity, poverty, and obedience." And it seems that this experience gets repeated for a lot of people.

What I chose to do was to become a social entrepreneur, which is a person who sets up an organization that does good works in the social sector. I did what I knew how to do based on my experience with my old company: I formed a team and got clear about a mission. The mission was to help pastors of large churches learn more about management. Most pastors aren't taught management in their academic preparation, so our organization found a way for them to be with people like Peter Drucker and Ken Blanchard and with themselves. Prison Fellowship is a result of a social entrepreneur. So is Habitat for Humanity. So is Focus on the Family. This is harder to do than it looks. So you have to bring your lunch and get over the comments people make to you like, "So, what exactly are you doing now?" That raises all sorts of insecurities in us, but it leads to the fifth and final rule that I experienced about going into the second half of my life, the half that leads to significance.

"What Would You Have Me Do?"

Rule five is that there must be a strong vision of an alternative future. If you are drawn away from something, you are drawn toward something. All of us understand that in a work context. Those of us who came out of college know it because we faced opportunities to do some things, which meant drawing us away from doing others. So if we solved it in our business-career lives, we can solve it in our ministry lives as well. All we have to do is say to God, "What would You have me do?" It is important to say that with sincerity and with open hands and hearts. All He wants is our availability.

I spoke about this topic at a large church recently, and a man approached me afterward and said, "What about us guys who aren't superstars? What about those of us who aren't world changers?" The answer that came to me comes right out of Scripture. I don't think God used world changers to accomplish His purposes in the Bible. Look at Abraham—a man of great faith who claimed his wife was his sister and offered her to the enemy! God used Peter, too. There's a guy who cut off a man's ear one minute while defending Jesus, and denied he knew Jesus the next minute. God has gotten a lot done with our squirrely selves.

"Don't worry," I told the man. "Make yourself available. God can still hit a long ball using a crooked bat." George Bernard Shaw said that true joy in life is

> being a force of nature instead of a feverish selfish little clod of ailments and grievances, complaining that the world will not devote itself to making you happy.... I want to be thoroughly used up when I die, for the harder I work, the more I live.... Life is not a brief candle for me. It is a sort of splendid torch which I've got a hold of for the moment, and I want to make it burn as brightly as possible before handing it on to future generations.

I believe that God calls us to play the entire game—both halves—and that by allowing Him to move us from desiring success to desiring significance, we best serve Him and the world He created.

Hank Brown is a man who has used all the talents that God has given him to weave a tapestry of success in his life. He worked his way through college, was student body president, Vietnam veteran, then a successful businessman, congressman, U.S. Senator, father, and husband.

My relationship to Hank goes back to his mom and my mom being in each other's weddings many years ago.

When Hank was young, his parents divorced. Hank's mom worked her way though law school and became the first woman attorney at Standard Oil. Later, she became the first female editor at Bancroft Whitney.

After finishing high school, Hank won a football scholarship to the University of Colorado. He lettered in wrestling and was elected student body president. He graduated with a degree in business and volunteered for the Navy.

Hank earned his commission at the Navy Officer Cadet School and volunteered for flight training. Completing training at Pensacola, Florida, and Corpus Christi, Texas, Hank earned his navigator wings. He served for two years in a VR squadron and then volunteered for service in Vietnam, flying as a forward air controller in an L-19. As a spotter, he located targets, marked them with smoke, and coordinated air strikes.

Hank became assistant to the president of Monfort of Colorado, the largest cattle feeder in the world. He became the youngest vice president in the company's history and went on to lead one of its larger divisions.

In 1980 Hank won a seat in the House of Representatives from Colorado's 4th congressional district and served five two-year terms, attaining an influential position on the House Ways and Means committee. He was then a U.S. Senator for six years.

Hank was so convinced of the importance of higher education and the need for expertise in his field that he spent his nights getting his master's degree in tax while serving in Congress, because he could be more knowledgeable as a member of the House Ways and Means committee. He also passed the C.P.A. exam on his first attempt while serving in Congress. It was also rumored that, vote after vote, Hank was the only Congressman who had read and studied every item before it hit the House floor for a vote.

Hank had the opportunity to help develop a major role for the University of Denver in international trade, and then the University of Northern Colorado at Greeley called him to be their president, a job he holds today.

13

The Role of Challenges in Our Lives

Hank Brown

LEADERSHIP IS ONE OF THOSE WORDS THAT everyone uses, but not everyone agrees on its definition. Some people believe leadership involves articulating a vision and then searching for a following. Christians believe leadership involves letting others see Christ at work through them.

Leadership involves listening to others. By listening, I mean actively seeking out what other people think about a subject, not just having the people closest to you tell you what they think you want to hear. Leadership begins with listening and thinking.

One of the misconceptions people have about leadership is that the leader has everything figured out and knows exactly where the organization is going. As a result, some have wrongly followed spiritual leaders who had simple answers to what it means to live in this world. For instance, some have taken the commandments that God gave Moses, and the admonition that Christ gave us to love one another, and have made them into a checklist for gaining prosperity in this temporal world. The thought is if we abide by the Ten Commandments, and if we do what Jesus told us to do, then God will reward us with earthly treasure and protect us from tragedy. But what is the purpose of our Maker's guidance for our lives? Is it to guide us toward prosperity in this world or the next?

The Tragedy at Columbine

The incomprehensible tragedy at Columbine High School in my home state is an example of a tragedy that will continue to affect, not only the families of the victims, but all of us for many years.

Next month it will be 46 years since my brother died in a gun accident. He was only 16—not much younger than the children who were murdered at Columbine. The other day my mother said to me that not a day goes by that she doesn't think of my brother and miss him. I suspect that the parents and loved ones of the victims at Columbine will be the same. The memory of those children will be with them every day for the rest of their lives. How do we explain it? How do you reconcile the tragedy in your own mind?

We believe our God is good; we believe our God is love; we believe our God is all-powerful and capable of controlling everything. How then could something this evil be allowed to happen? It's not a new question. It's been with mankind throughout history.

The Story of Job

A few thousand years ago, Job had the same question. He was devout, religious, and pious. He was committed to carrying on the work of the Lord, yet great tragedies were visited upon him. He lost his home. He lost his fortune. He lost his health. He even lost his beloved children. But he didn't lose his faith. And throughout it, he asked "Why?"

Was he being tested? Was he being punished? I'm not sure we know. His friends suggested that he must be being punished, that he must have done something wrong. And yet, Job was a righteous man. He hadn't been evil; he hadn't sinned. He'd kept the faith. The attitude of Job's friends is perhaps parallel to the way many of us think. It's natural to think that if we're good, if we follow the rules, if we observe the mandates, good things will happen to us. And yes, if we sin, we'll be punished. And yet, Job hadn't sinned. I don't pretend to know the answer. But I want to suggest that part of the answer lies in God's purpose for our lives in this world.

What if this earthly existence is not intended to be a paradise? What if our Maker's real kingdom is not of this world? What if the purpose of our earthly existence is to train us, to prepare us, to test us—not for this world, but for the next? What if the commandments of Moses and the admonition to love each other aren't on a checklist for prosperity in this world, but are guidance for how we'll behave when we truly accept grace? Not a way to earn grace, but a prescription for how we'll live if we accept grace. What if those commandments are the best advice in history on how to live a joyous life and find happiness on earth? If this is so, then our earthly existence may not be about earning our way to heaven or even enjoying a perfect life on earth. It may be about learning and preparing for the next life.

Preparing Our Children

Everyday parents face something of the challenge that our Lord must experience. How do you prepare children for life? We love our children more than life itself. But do we do their homework for them? If we don't help them with their homework, they may fail and may not have the chances we hope for them. But if we do their homework for them, what do they learn? How do they learn that they have to prepare in advance for the next challenge? How have we helped them learn a lesson for life?

Growing up, I couldn't understand my mother. How could she be so tough? She never once bought the stories I brought home about how everyone did it, how it must be okay because everyone else got by with it. In fact, she was never even tempted by them. I recall a series of incidents of her forcing me to confess my sins—once to a storeowner from whose store I'd taken some gum, once to my grandmother, and once at school. Those forced confessions resulted in unbelievable embarrassment. How could she do such a thing? If I wanted something, her answer was, "I'll help you find a job." I worked 20-40 hours a week while I was in high school; and in the summers I had one or two full-time jobs, depending on the summer. My parents were divorced. Mom worked full-time. She didn't have a lot of time to supervise me. But her strategy was to keep me busy, and she kept me so busy I almost stayed out of trouble. As I look back, I wonder whether I have been near as good a parent as she was.

"He Was the One Who Loved Me Most"

I will never forget the Clarence Thomas hearings—I was serving in the United States Senate then. I recall a question posed by one of my colleagues—a person of great integrity—who had very strong doubts about Clarence Thomas' judicial philosophy. When his turn came to ask questions, the senator said to Mr. Thomas, "I see two Clarence Thomases, not just one. I see one that seems so kind, generous, thoughtful, and warm. And then I see one that is mean, cruel, and hard. Which one are you?"

Justice Thomas responded immediately. He said, "There is only one Clarence Thomas, and I am he. I used to wonder how my uncle could pretend to care for me so much and be so hard on me. It wasn't until later in life that I learned that he was the one who loved me the most. He loved me enough to prepare me for the challenges ahead." I wonder if our Lord has in mind to prepare us for a life to come.

Could tragedies and trials in this life help prepare us for the next? It's a question worth asking. The year my brother died, I was 13. My grandfather gave me a book by Woodrow Wilson, a wonderful little book called *When a Man Comes to Himself*. It had as strong an influence on me as any book I've read. Wilson, as you may know, was an idealist. In the book he talks about the true joys in life. He observes that the real pay one gets from a job isn't the paycheck at the end of the month, although that's important. The real joy comes from what you do. A bricklayer or carpenter can drive through town and see the homes he's built that provide shelter and warmth for families. Others could look at the work they've done and see how it impacts lives and changes the people they know. Wilson's thesis was that you are what you do with your life. He believed that you are the role you play among your fellows. If that's true, it's worthwhile for us to ask ourselves from time to time what our life is amounting to.

Wilson's thought was that we are the sum total of how we help each other and the role we play amongst others. Perhaps that's a good guide for us to evaluate what we do in life. It's also a pretty good guide to examine as to whether you've found the real joy in life. I don't know the answer to Job's question. Like you, the events and the currents of evil in he world trouble me. Like you, I suspect that our responsibility is to do what we can to prevent tragedy. I'm not sure there's a surefire formula by which we can do that, but I do believe that the freedom God gives us to live our lives and make our choices surely must be designed to prepare us for another world and help us understand that we have a role in making this world better.

Will Perkins was born and raised in Colorado Springs where he still lives with his wife of 50 years, Bess. After graduating from Colorado College, Will played baseball in the Chicago White Sox minor league before joining his father's Chrysler/Plymouth dealership. After his father's sudden death, Will took over leadership of the business.

I remember that, every Christmas, Will would buy advertising time on the local television stations and talk about the Christmas story and the baby Jesus—not about cars, trucks, and vans. His success as a businessman led to his being elected to two terms as president of the national Chrysler/Plymouth advisory council, the only dealer to have that distinction.

When Colorado Springs was looking for a chairman of the committee to be formed to attract parachurch ministries to relocate their world headquarters to Colorado Springs, they chose Will. As a result of that effort, as of January 1, 2000, there are more than 150 ministries or Christian organizations with their world headquarters in Colorado Springs.

Will and Bess have three daughters and a son, who is now the president of the family Chrysler dealership. All the kids are married and have supplied Will and Bess with 12 grandchildren. In the years I've known him, Will Perkins has shown himself to be a man of consistency, a man who walks his talk as a Christian businessman.

14

Understanding Your Condition

Will Perkins

THE FIRST TIME I CONSCIOUSLY AFFIRMED MY belief in God was in a geology class in college. The professor said that we were going to talk about how the world began, and that we students had a choice. If we wanted to study it from the perspective of creationism, we were told to take a theology class. If we wanted to study it from the perspective of evolution, then we should stay in that professor's class. I stayed.

But by the end of the semester, I realized that it would take more faith to believe that all of this just happened than it would to think that a Creator designed it. So I decided to go with God. It wasn't what I would call a conversion experience, but a decision that believing in God made more sense than not believing in Him. There were just too many gaps in how evolution was explained.

I graduated in 1950, and by 1958 I was married with three children. Within a few years of our marriage, my wife, Bess, began encouraging me to attend a weekly Bible study with her. I had no interest, however. I was a salesman, not a preacher. However, at my house, if my wife thinks I should do something, it isn't very long before I also think it would be a good idea to do whatever she thinks I should. So one night I agreed to go with her. I even found the old Bible that my grandfather had given me when I graduated from high school. It was in perfect condition. The group was looking at John, chapter 3, where a rabbi named Nicodemus asked Jesus what he had to do to have eternal life. Jesus told him that he needed to be born again. Nicodemus was puzzled by this and asked, "How can a man be born when he is old?...Surely he cannot enter a second time into his mother's womb to be born!" (verse 4). Jesus then explained what it meant to be born again.

The discussion at the Bible study then turned to the topic of eternity, about who was going to heaven, and who was going to hell. I remember looking around the room, and recognizing a lot of the people there. I thought to myself, *I'm better than a lot of the people in this room, and yet I don't know whether I'm going to heaven. That just doesn't seem right.* So after the meeting I approached Doug Sparks, the Bible study leader, and told him that I attended the largest church in town, but I didn't understand what they had been talking about all evening. Doug asked me, "Will, do you believe in God?"

"Of course!" I replied. I had never even considered that God might not exist.

"Do you believe you're a sinner?" Doug continued.

I hadn't really thought about it quite that way. As a matter of fact, that's a lousy question to ask a used-car salesman! I told him that I knew I wasn't perfect, but I thought I was better than a lot of people I knew. I assumed that God graded on a curve, and that as long as I was in the top 50 percent of the population, I was in good shape. I was comparing my life to my peers and friends and looking pretty good.

Then Doug showed me Romans 3:23, which says, "For all have sinned and fall short of the glory of God." When he read that, I knew that I was in trouble. Next he turned to Romans 6:23, which says, "For the wages of sin is death, but the gift of God is eternal life." That meant my future in heaven wasn't as sure a thing as I had thought. Here was the Bible telling me that I was a sinner, and unless I became born again, I wasn't going to spend eternity with Jesus. The next verse he showed me was Romans 5:8, which says, "But God demonstrates his own love for us in this: While we were still sinners, Christ died for us."

This was just amazing to me. This was way beyond believing in God, the way I had been for years. This was something else, something deeper. I knew that Jesus had died for the sins of the world, but I had never thought about how it affected me. Doug then showed me Revelation 3:20, which says, "Here I am! I stand at the door and knock. If anyone hears my voice and opens the door, I will come in and eat with him, and he with me." Finally, we looked at the first few verses of John that show the Word was with us from the beginning, and the Word was Jesus, and that Jesus is God.

I remember saying, "What? Jesus is God? I've gone to church all my life, and I never knew that!"

Doug then asked, "Will, would you like to accept Christ as your Savior right here and enter into a personal relationship with God beyond your intellectual knowledge of Him? You could pray right now."

I hadn't prayed much in my life. I had been an athlete while I was growing up, and even played baseball for the Chicago White Sox. The only time I prayed was in the ninth inning when I was at bat, or in the last seconds of a basketball game when I was taking a jump shot. The way I practiced it, I didn't think prayer was very effective.

I told the Bible study leader that I would think about it, and went home.

I Assumed I Was a Christian

That night I gave this conversation a lot of thought. It was all very confusing to me, because I had been born in America and had gone to church for years and believed in

God, so I assumed I was a Christian. But the Bible showed me that I was not.

Later that night, when everyone was asleep, I went down to our basement. I didn't want anyone to see me do what I was about to do. I wanted to believe that what I had been shown that night was true, so I said to God, "I don't know if I'm a Christian or not. If I'm not, I want to be." Then I grabbed onto a chair and waited for it to hit me. Nothing did. Nothing felt different. I went to bed thinking I had been sold a bill of goods.

The next week my life was the same as the week before. Nothing had changed—except that I wanted to go back to that Bible study. Surprisingly, the discussion that night was more interesting to me than the week before. Later, Doug asked me if I had given last week's conversation any thought. I told him what I had done, and that I was disappointed. He turned in his Bible to the same verses from Revelation and read, "If *anyone* opens the door..."

"Did you invite Christ to come into your life?" he asked.

"Yes, I did," I replied.

"Did He come in?" he asked.

"I guess so," I answered.

"How do you know?" he asked.

"Because it says so in the Bible," I said.

"Perkins," he said with a grin, "congratulations! You just learned an important lesson. You can't depend on your feelings; they can fool you. But you can trust God's Word."

Doug started another regular Bible study with some other men who had made decisions for Christ at about the same time. During one of these studies he compared the promises of God to deposits in the bank. If someone deposits money in my account but doesn't tell me, I won't know that I can write checks against it. The promises in the Bible are deposited in our accounts, he explained. We can only access them when we are aware of them. By inviting Christ into my life, it was like I became aware of the gift of eternal life that God had provided in my "bank account." My feelings had nothing to do with a decision to access that account.

Within a couple of weeks I asked my wife if she had ever heard about being in a personal relationship with God. She immediately began to cry, and explained that she had heard someone claim that Jesus Christ was as real to her as anyone in that room. Bess had then prayed and asked God that if He really existed, would He prompt me to ask Bess about Him. Although we attended church faithfully, Bess and I never discussed God. My asking her this question confirmed her faith. As a result, we began our Christian walk together. We started praying together, specifically for our children. Soon, with our new faith in Christ, we became centered on God's love, which was a dimension our lives didn't have before.

Reading the Owner's Manual

As I became more familiar with God's Word, I saw that biblical principles apply not just to our personal home life, but also to our business life and every other aspect of life as well. When we sell someone a new car at our dealership, we provide them with an owner's manual. This manual was prepared under the supervision of the people who designed the car. If you do what they suggest, you'll experience the full potential of your new car. However, you don't have to pay attention to what this manual says. All you have to do is put gas in the car, and you can drive it any way you please. But if you ignore the advice of the manufacturer, in a short time you'll have problems that could have been avoided. God created life and He provided a way to communicate with us through the Holy Scriptures. As the Designer, He tells us how to get the best out of life. However, He gives us the option of ignoring His advice and living any way we choose. One day, though, there will be an accounting for the way we've lived. The effects of our choices will be made evident.

For me, this didn't seem like a problem as long as I compared my life to other people. God graded on a curve, I thought, and I certainly was in the top half of the class. As such, I didn't consider sin a big problem. But then I read in Acts 17:31 that God will judge the world by the standard of Jesus Christ.

Shortly thereafter, the sin in my life was made real to me through an experience that helped me understand how sin can sneak up on us. I was driving down a mountain highway and began having car trouble. I pulled over to the shoulder, lifted the hood, checked all of the obvious things, and then concluded that I had a flat tire! While I was changing it, a truck with an awful stench passed me. It was a rendering truck that hauled away dead animals from the side of the road.

After I finished changing my tire and was on my way again, I began to catch up to the truck. The closer I got, the stronger the stench became. I could hardly breathe. I was sure the driver of the truck must be wearing a gas mask. When I got alongside the driver, I looked over at him, and not only did he *not* have something to block the smell, he was actually smiling!

It dawned on me that sin is like that. It's bad, but you get used to it. Only when we're made aware of it do we realize our condition. The Bible tells us that our righteousness is as filthy rags. But God said that if we would come to Him, He would clean us up and replace our filthiness and stench with His righteousness. Furthermore, this offer was a free gift of God to anyone who realized his plight and was willing for God to come into his life.

The Odometer Problem

As I became more sensitive to God's presence in my life, I began to evaluate our automobile dealership from a biblical perspective. One practice that we engaged in bothered me quite a bit. Our service department performed a metamorphic procedure on used cars similar to that of a butterfly. A car would come in with 60,000 miles on it and leave with 30,000. In those days, odometer laws were practically nonexistent. My dad and I were partners in the business, and I explained my concern about this practice to him. He said that he didn't like it either; however, to remain in the used-car business, we had to do it because everybody else did. He reminded me that we guaranteed the car as though it had adjusted mileage, so it really wasn't so bad. This was true, and I explained it that way to God and concluded my prayer by reminding God that although my dad and I were partners, my dad was really the boss.

Not long after this, my dad was suddenly stricken with a fatal heart attack. I was with him in the hospital. I held my arm around him and rubbed his left arm. Then I asked him, "Dad, have you turned everything over to the Lord?" He answered, "I sure have." He took a deep breath and left this world to be with his Savior.

Now I had no partner. I spent the next several months trying to figure out how to handle this mileage thing. I went to meetings with other dealers and asked them what they did. They all answered the same: They didn't like it, but they did it.

Finally, I told God I was no longer going to turn back odometers on newly arriving used cars. If He wanted me in the car business, He would have to take care of the problem. I called the staff at our dealership together and said we were ending the practice of setting back odometers. Surprisingly, they said they agreed with me.

They agreed until we began losing business. It's a simple reality that you can't get as much money for a car with 60,000 miles as you can for a car with 30,000 miles. It was tempting to go back to the old ways, but we hung in there and the Lord took care of us. We're still in business 40 years later, and I've been elected chairman of the National Chrysler Dealers' Council twice.

Work as Ministry

Something else becoming a Christian did in regard to my business is that it helped me look at work as more than just a job. Working—earning a living every day—is a drag. But if you are a Christian, God intends for you to use your job as a ministry—as a way to show the world that Jesus is Lord. With that knowledge, we can look forward to every day because we know that the Lord is going to do something through us. I look at 1 Corinthians 15:58 as the foundation for this approach to work: "Therefore, my dear brothers, stand firm. Let nothing move you. Always give yourself fully to the work of the Lord, because you know that your labor in the Lord is not in vain." That's our motivation. When we look at our work as a ministry instead of just a way to make a living, God adds a wonderful dimension to our days.

One of the most difficult lessons I have learned as a Christian and a businessman is that God does not promise us success. A few years ago I was convinced that God wanted me to run for mayor of Colorado Springs. It defied all reason, and my close friends and advisers told me it was a crazy idea. They all knew that I didn't have any political savvy or support. But I was convinced that God wanted me to do it, so I was firm with my friends and family that I was going ahead with the campaign.

I lost that election. And on election night I was the happiest guy in town—not because I had lost, but because I had been faithful to God's call on my life. As a former baseball and basketball player, I knew that God didn't always guarantee His followers a victory on every contest. All He asks is that we look to Him for direction and give it our best shot. I still don't know why He wanted me to run for mayor. I only know that He did, and that I was obedient. It taught me yet another lesson: His call on our lives doesn't mean we're going to be at the top of the heap. It just means that He goes with us and before us along the way.

I'm a survivor in a very tough business. I sold my first car when I was 16 years old. It was a pea-green DeSoto four-door sedan. I have sold a lot of cars since then. But other people have made a lot more money than I have. *Financial success* is a subjective term. I know that God has provided everything I have needed and more. The reason I'm content with how my business has gone comes from Colossians 2. It describes how I have tried to live my life as a Christian businessman: "So then, just as you received Christ Jesus as Lord, continue to live in him, rooted and built up in him, strengthened in the faith as you were taught, and overflowing with thankfulness. See to it that no one takes you captive through hollow and deceptive philosophy, which depends on human tradition and the basic principles of this world rather than on Christ" (verses 6-8).

Since I found Christ, my job has been a springboard to ministry. I believe that God calls us to live under His influence in all that we do—especially at work.

More than 20 years ago I met a banker from Chicago who had come to Colorado to help a large Denver bank put together a line of credit for one of their largest clients. That banker was Sam Addoms, and he ended up being hired by that Colorado company as its chief financial officer.

Sam left that role after several years of helping to turn the company into a very strong leader in its industry. He went on to become involved in several different companies in Colorado, including Frontier Airlines, where he serves as president and CEO.

Sam has turned out to be such a tremendous leader for Frontier that, after six years in business, Frontier has more than 1200 employees with flights out of Denver, their hub, to the West Coast, East Coast, and many flights north and south.

Sam and his wife, Cathy, live in Denver where they have become very involved in the community. Cathy writes one or two recipes every month for the *Frontier* magazine.

15

A Map, a Compass, and a Rudder

Sam Addoms

AT FIRST GLANCE, THE PRINCIPLES OF AVIATION don't seem to have much in common with the principles of life, but more and more, I think they do. For example, to fly and to live you need to know where you're going and how to get there successfully. A pilot needs a map. So does a person who wants to live his life fully, in the way God intended it to be lived. A pilot also needs a compass. Every flight and every life needs something that will set the course so that you know you're going in the right direction. And both a pilot and a person need a rudder—something by which to steer. I have seen all three of these necessary guides at work in my life and in the company called Frontier Airlines.

I became involved with the airline in its earliest stages. A former president of the original Frontier Airlines called and invited me to join with other associates of his to begin a new airline, also to be named Frontier Airlines.

"We don't need any financing for this project—it's all spoken for," he assured me. Although I was busy running a computer software company at the time, I told him I was willing to be involved in financial planning using my weekend and evening spare time.

My first meeting with the former president and his other associates took place at a small airport outside of Denver. When the meeting had concluded, I noticed that no one had said a word about money. I raised my hand and said, "No one has spoken about financing this venture. Where is the money coming from?"

"It's all been arranged," they told me.

"But who is the person giving us this money?" I asked.

There was a long pause. No one could remember his name.

"Do we have the name on file somewhere?" I asked.

A fellow raced off to look in a file and, after a few minutes, brought back the business card of a man located in Israel.

"Do you suppose I could call him up and confirm that we've got something?" I asked.

"Sure," they said.

So I called the man and said, "I understand that you've discussed financing Frontier Airlines."

"Yes, I'm very interested," he said. "Send me the business plan."

"How much investment do you contemplate for this company?" I asked.

"I don't contemplate anything. That's why I want to read the business plan," he answered very businesslike. "All I agreed to do was read the business plan."

"So you aren't prepared to put any money in the company?" I asked.

"Of course not," he answered. "I wouldn't put money in an airline if it were the last investment out there. I know some guys who are dumb enough to do it though."

That was my real introduction to Frontier Airlines.

Riding the Tailwind

That fall I sold the computer software company and took the finalized Frontier Airlines business plan home to my wife. We looked it over and I said, "Let's give this six months and see if we can get it funded." If it didn't work by then, we would know that the time had been spent in "creative unemployment."

It was at this point that I witnessed the power of prayer in acquiring the company's map and compass. It was a remarkable example of the unmistakable direction available from God. During this time of transition, we received a call from some members of a prayer group that met each week on Friday evening. They were former Frontier employees, and every week part of their prayer time was devoted to asking for God's direction in the future of that company. They explained that our efforts to start this airline with the Frontier name was in answer to their prayers.

Wow! With a tailwind like that, I knew we couldn't go wrong. It was a profound experience. And, of course, when we took the plan around to the investment community, we got the financing required to begin.

Soon we were in business. We sent our first five planes to Montana and North Dakota. Almost as quickly we discovered that while those are beautiful, scenic states, they're also states with small populations. At this time, the wife of Frontier's founding CEO became terminally ill. He and his wife would move back to their home in Arizona. I felt as if the map, the compass, and the rudder for the company were all leaving at once. For a while, he tried to run the company by telephone from Arizona, but that's difficult to do even if a company is doing well. And we were not doing well.

The Unfriendly Skies

We approached the leader of one of the country's largest airlines and proposed a passenger partnership. We suggested that since his aircraft fly into Denver frequently, perhaps our system of going to smaller cities could work well with his system. We could take his passengers on to our smaller airports, and our passengers could arrange to travel to their destination. It seemed like a good idea. But when I finished my proposal, the man rose out of his chair, jammed his knuckles on his desk, and asked, "Why would we do anything with you?"

It was back to the drawing board. For several months we sought direction through trial and error. Eventually our CEO decided that his long-distance arrangement wasn't working. Upon his resignation, I was named CEO. But the company was floundering—we were lost.

Then one day a young man came by to introduce himself and said, "I'm a marketing guy. You're flying to all the wrong cities. You should fly into big cities and charge low fares. If you want, I'll show you how to do it." It was like the carpenter had showed up just in time to build the staircase.

We began flying to big cities, charged low fares, and started making money. It was salvation for our 600 employees, and for two consecutive quarters we made a profit. But then the big airline we had met with before came down on us like a house of fire. A federal excise tax was renewed, which required that we pay the federal government ten percent of our ticket price. In our business, that was a lot of money. We figured we would just raise our ticket prices by the ten percent, and assumed all the other airlines would do the same. We were wrong. This particular large airline appeared to raise their fares in the 52 markets that we weren't in. In fact, in some markets, they raised them even more than ten percent. But they didn't raise them in the markets that we shared. The effect was as if someone hooked up a hose to our bank account and pumped our cash out the window. It was that dramatic.

People in the industry told us not to do anything. "Don't say anything," they advised us. "Stay down. Eventually they'll stop doing this. But don't make a big deal out of it."

So we did the opposite. We wrote a book called *The Unfriendly Skies Over Colorado*, and called a press conference in Denver. We said things like, "The vampire can't stand the light of day." Pretty heavy rhetoric! We visited the Department of Justice and the Department of Transportation. We gave them a 20-year history of airline deregulation and the difficulties it created for new carriers. The fact that 200 carriers had been born and 190 had died was pretty revealing evidence, we thought.

Two months after our Washington trip, the airline stopped its predatory practice against us. We had no expectations that we might accomplish anything in Washington, but I was thrilled. The company was saved. Of course I assumed it was our lobbying that had done it.

But a few months later I was meeting with an associate who runs an investment banking firm. I told him this story and he was very happy for us. Then he told me his own story. He is a friend of the CEO of the airline we had been battling, and they had been in Aspen skiing together during the time I was in Washington trying to get the government to help us out. He said that he and the CEO had dinner together with their wives after a full day on the slopes, and as the appetizers arrived he asked, "Why is your company behaving in a predatory, anticompetitive manner toward Frontier Airlines?"

The CEO replied, "What?"

My associate went on to describe what was happening at Frontier, and told the CEO that his company might put Frontier out of business. At this point, the CEO's wife turned to her husband and said, "Honey, we don't do *that*, do we?" So much for Washington D.C.! I can just picture that CEO returning to the office and pulling the plug on the Kill Frontier Department! No matter how it happened, I had a real sense that God had pulled us back from the brink.

And though God is in the rescue business, some people view their relationship with God as just a means of bailing them out of trouble. That hasn't been my own experience. In my relationship with Him, I feel as if I am in constant dialogue. Daily prayer and thanksgiving have been my compass. My map has been to continuously seek God's will and invoke the phrase, "Thy will be done." That frees me up from having to accomplish everything myself. I just want to bring my life and the company's life under the direction of God's will, continually giving them back to Him. It sounds easy, but believe me, it's not.

Soon after we got out from under the problem with one airline, we encountered trouble from another. This was a smaller carrier. They announced to us that they were moving into Denver. They were bigger, faster, flashier, had more publicity, and had raised (and spent) a lot of cash—140 million dollars. We had raised only about 30 million dollars by then.

Trying to work out a deal with them looked like the difference between staying in business or dying, so we agreed to merge. We combined schedules and created a system where our jets would take passengers from point A to point B, and theirs would take them on to point C. People needed only one ticket for this, and the service was expected to be consistent throughout the trip—or so we thought.

There were financial problems with this new arrangement from the beginning. The other airline made financial forecasts that they just couldn't meet. They were consistently five million dollars behind each month. They had said that once they got into the Denver market with us, their profit picture would improve.

Bag Heaven

It soon became evident why they weren't making money. For one thing, they didn't think about being on time. It was more of a casual thing with them. Also, they had something called "Bag Heaven," where passengers' luggage went. We discovered "Bag Heaven" when we visited their home-office facility in Colorado Springs. A room was completely filled with lost luggage.

Here's how our dialogue went:

"What are you doing about these bags?" we asked.

"We don't have to do anything about these bags," they said.

We were horrified.

"Why don't you have to do anything about them?" we asked.

"The people who lost them will write us a letter and ask for the bag back."

"What happens when they write the letter?"

"We find the bag and send it back."

"What if you can't find the bag?"

"We write them a letter and tell them to send their receipts for everything they had in their bag."

"What happens next?"

"They send us the receipts."

"How much does it cost to handle a claim?"

"It doesn't cost anything."

"Why doesn't it cost anything?"

"We don't pay the claim."

"What?"

"We make them write another letter."

"Why?"

"So we can send them another letter that says the check is in the mail."

"That check costs you money."

"No it doesn't. We don't even tell the accounting office to send the check. We make the passenger send us another letter."

I couldn't believe what I was hearing. The airline business is a service industry that's completely dependent on three things: being on time, reliability of baggage handling, and friendliness. And this company was our partner.

Within a few weeks of this exchange we called the other airline and said the deal wasn't working. The discussions to end the partnership were as acrimonious and bitter as any I can recall in my business experience. They said things like, "We're going to seek protection in bankruptcy, and we're going to kill you." To add insult to injury, they got an investor to put up another 50 million dollars to keep them flying, which I just couldn't believe. We had never seen that kind of money.

Hope Renewed

It really did appear that they were going to bury us. But then something occurred to me that I can attribute to God's direction. Remember, I'm not the kind of guy who senses God saying, "Do this, do that." I just have this running dialogue with Him, and I keep asking that His will be done. But it seemed very clear to me that this company's forecast with this new investor was probably as shaky as the one they gave us when they wanted to be our partner. So we started counting the number of passengers they had on their planes and saw that they were running at about 35 percent capacity. This was well below their plan and a figure that would have any airline executive jumping out of his window even if he was on the first floor! My hopes for Frontier were renewed.

And we were right about their faulty forecasts. Eventually their investor saw the reality, too, and pulled back. We have since become the principal provider of low-cost air service in our region, and have been consistently profitable since then.

This entire experience showed me the importance of depending on God for our map. His will became the map. Continually giving the company and my life over to His will hasn't been easy, but it's kept us confident that God was in everything we were doing.

Daily prayer and thanksgiving have been the compass. If we have the map, this is the way we can set the more specific direction of our lives. Prayer and thanksgiving contribute to our directional accuracy.

The steering mechanism for our lives—the rudder—is the collective consciousness of those around us. God uses our friends, our family, our teachers, our mentors, our failures, and our successes to steer us in the way we should go next. Clearly, God is in our conscience and in our personal reflection, but He also guides by using other people. That's how He has worked in my life.

During my most difficult times as a businessman, the Lord's Prayer became my prayer. It was a core part of that dialogue that kept me on the map. I have found that simply having a conversation with God, using that prayer as the focus, allows me to describe my state of mind to Him and to ask for direction. It's the most powerful thing I can do. It helps me turn everything over to Him, and it makes the outcome His. I feel that I am an instrument in His hands.

Bill Armstrong is a gifted businessman who, while still in his 20s, was asked to run for the Colorado state legislature. He won that election and served as a state senator before winning a Congressional seat in 1972. He later ran for and won a U.S. Senate seat, where he served for 12 years. It was while Bill was serving in the United States Senate that he became a Christian through the witness of a man he had never previously met. In 1991, Bill returned to private life, where he immersed himself in a Colorado real estate and mortgage company.

I first met Bill at a political outing when he declared himself as a candidate for the Colorado state senate. I believed then and I still believe we need more businesspeople in politics—people like Bill. As a result of Bill's efforts to encourage more businessmen to be involved in the process, Colorado has a large number of people from the business sector involved in politics, locally and nationally.

Bill and Ellen Armstrong have a grown son and daughter, and both his son and son-in-law are in business with him in Colorado.

16

God Calls Us to Participate

William Armstrong

AT THE BEGINNING OF THE TWENTY-FIRST century, America remains the preeminent world power. Our country is, by any reasonable definition, the richest, most progressive, and the freest of the world's largest countries. We're number one in technology, business, science, medicine, and much more. In some ways, America's prospects have never been brighter.

Unfortunately, this country is also a world leader in drug abuse, violence, abortion, and pornography. The greatness of America is relentlessly undermined by racial strife, political corruption, cynicism, and the breakup of families. There is an odor of decadence in the air.

Such issues, along with many others, were on my mind when I ran for election to the United States Congress. In the nation's capital, I found men and women from all over America who had similar concerns. Republicans, Democrats, liberals, conservatives—we had vastly different ideas about public policy, but we all shared a belief in the future of America and a desire to preserve everything good about our country and make it an even better place for our children and grandchildren.

I had the privilege of closely working with many talented, outstanding, dedicated, celebrated men and women in Congress, the Cabinet, the White House, and the federal courts for nearly two decades. Interestingly, however, I don't know of one of them who would say that within their vocations they had discovered the answers to the deepest questions of life. I don't know of a general or an admiral who would say he had a military strategy that responded to the innermost needs of the human heart, or a senator, congressman, businessman, or economist who would make a similar claim for economic theory or political strategy.

On the other hand, I know many—perhaps hundreds—of these celebrated men and women who would solemnly testify, as do I, that you can't find the answers to what's really important in life through military strategy, economics, political science, or any theory. They would affirm with me that you can't find the answers to life's deepest questions except in a relationship with the Person of Jesus Christ.

One of these noted men was Dr. Charles Malik, a Lebanese statesman, educator, and diplomat. A noted scholar, Dr. Malik received honorary degrees from more than 50 universities around the world, was a signer of the original United Nations charter, and served as Lebanon's delegate to the United Nations for ten years. Near the end of his long life, this great Christian man put into words what many people in public and private life have concluded: The deepest needs of the world go far beyond political freedom and economic justice, far beyond sociology and politics. Dr. Malik said the deepest needs of the world belong to the sphere of the mind, the heart, and the spirit—a sphere to be penetrated with the light and grace of Jesus Christ.

Someone else I deeply admire put it even more simply—a California man who closed up his business in Los Angeles and went on to become a celebrated author and a world traveler. A man who has been all over the world, has visited every continent except Antarctica, and has established friendships with people in every walk of life: presidents, prime ministers, parliamentarians, prisoners, homemakers, students. This man, with a great heart and a vast reservoir of wisdom and experience, put it even more simply than Dr. Malik. He said, "If we are going to change the world, we must first change men's hearts. And only Jesus Christ can change men's hearts."

How is this a leadership principle? It seems to me that one of the requirements for leadership is to show people where they can find the answers to their questions. In this case, it's showing them where to find the answers to the most important questions.

Money, Position, and Power

For me, this is an important issue because, although I had gone to church all my life, and my parents were Christians and my grandfather was a minister, I myself was not a Christian as I began to assume leadership roles in business and politics. I really had no interest in spiritual things. My life wasn't centered on Jesus Christ or on eternal values. It centered on being president of radio station KOSI. It centered on money, position, and power. My understanding was that to be successful, you had to have a lot of money, you had to own your own business, you had to join the country club, and so on. So I set out with a relentless determination to do exactly that.

The radio business interested me, so when I graduated from high school, I went into radio and worked all over the country. By the time I was 21, I had been just about everywhere and had done a lot of things in business. Then I found myself in Denver, Colorado, where I made a business transaction that a subsequent generation of entrepreneurs would call a "leveraged buyout." I had never heard that term before, but knew I wanted to buy the radio station. I also knew there was only one party in this transaction who had any money, and that was the seller. So I used his money to buy the company. It was a business my family and I ended up owning for nearly 25 years.

Soon there was a second station, followed by a weekly newspaper, and later a daily newspaper. It wasn't long before I began serving on some corporate boards. By the time I was 25 and on the verge of being married, a man came to call on me and my fiancée, Ellen (who has now been my wife for more than 38 years). The man asked me a surprising question: "Bill, how would you like to run for the state legislature?" I didn't know anything about the state legislature, so naturally I said, "Yes, I would be happy to do that."

I had no real knowledge of politics and knew nothing about the legislature. But one week to the day before Ellen and I were to be married, I went down to the political convention of my party in Colorado and imposed upon a man whom I had never met prior to that day. I asked him to place my name before the convention. On the strength of his reputation, I was designated to run in the primary election.

The following weekend, Ellen and I got married and went on our honeymoon. When we came back, I began to run in the primary and, amazingly, I won. I went on to win the general election and served in the Colorado house of representatives for two years. Then I ran for the state senate and served there for eight years. By that time I was 35 years old. All the while I was building my business, pursuing my ambitions, and Ellen and I had two wonderful kids we were busily raising.

Elected to Congress

After spending a decade in the Colorado legislature, I decided it was time to withdraw from public life and go back into business full-time. But just as I was making this decision, the census came along and a new district was created in the U. S. House of Representatives. I threw my hat in the ring, and the good people of the Fifth Congressional District elected me to go to Washington to represent them as a member of the House.

Can you imagine how I felt? By then I had reached all my goals. I had set a target of how much money I wanted to make by the time I was 30 years old and had achieved that. I had a fine family, a nice house, some businesses, and had served on some boards. Now I had been elected to the U.S. Congress, to go to Washington and whisper advice in the ear of the president of the United States. Fortunately, he did have a couple of other sources of advice, as well. But can you imagine how it felt inside to have achieved this level of success?

I felt great, right? Actually, it didn't happen that way. My experience was exactly the opposite. Even though I had achieved all the things I had dreamed of, the things I knew were important and counted for success, I still didn't feel successful. In fact, I felt terrible. Inside I was crumbling. On the outside, everything seemed fine: wonderful family, children, success in business, and success in politics. Inside, however, I was despondent.

A Stranger's Question

That was my frame of mind when a man came to call on me. He was not a clergyman or a constituent—just a dentist from Alabama who came to call on me at my office in the Cannon House Office Building. He asked me a completely unexpected and somewhat confrontational question. He asked, "Bill, where do you stand with Jesus Christ?"

I don't know about you, but where I come from that's not a question we ask people. The last thing we would do is to go over to someone and say, "How's everything between you and Jesus?" And we particularly don't go visit people in their offices and raise that kind of question, especially with perfect strangers.

In retrospect, it's interesting how this situation turned out because his question was a little embarrassing—and congressmen know how to get themselves out of embarrassing situations. I had a perfect opportunity to terminate this conversation because, as we were talking, the bells rang and the lights on my wall lit up to signify a vote was about to occur in the House of Representatives. All I had to do was say to this guy, "Look, I've got to vote. Thanks for dropping in. I'm going to go do my duty and go across the street to cast my vote."

But for reasons I didn't understand, but which now are absolutely clear, I didn't say that. Instead, I said, "I've got to vote. Walk over with me, and then we'll go down to the coffee shop, drink a cup of coffee, and continue to talk." So that's what we did. I voted, and then we went down into the Joseph Martin Dining Room, which is a little chamber under the House of Representatives. This dear guy, who was then a stranger but as you can now imagine has become a wonderful friend, shared with me a little pamphlet called "The Four Spiritual Laws."

I had never heard of "The Four Spiritual Laws," but I have since become very familiar with this publication. It's published by Campus Crusade for Christ and more than a billion copies have been printed, I'm told, in 120 languages around the world. But I had never heard of it.

"...There Are Also Spiritual Laws..."

I didn't know that "The Four Spiritual Laws" represented the distilled essence of the New Testament's teaching about man's relationship to God. Nevertheless, this dentist began to tell me about "The Four Spiritual Laws." He said, "Bill, if you want to get your life on track, if you would like to have the sort of relationship with God that the Bible says He longs to have with you, you've got to follow the spiritual laws of the universe. Just as there are physical laws—such as the laws of physics that govern the physical universe—there are also spiritual laws that govern our spiritual lives." So we sat down side by side and he opened this little pamphlet and began to read. As he read, he moved his finger under each word of this little pamphlet. (Evidently he thought congressmen didn't read very well!)

He said, "There are four things you need to understand. First, God loves you and has a wonderful plan for your life." Now I had been going to church all my life and I had heard of the love of God, so we didn't spend a lot of time on that. But he pointed out it was documented, citing some Bible verses to prove it.

Then he went on to the second spiritual law. He said, "Bill, there is something about you and every other human being that makes it impossible for you to have the kind of relationship with God that you would like to have. This something is what the Bible calls 'sin'!" I had heard of sin, but had never thought of it in connection with myself. But at least I had heard of sin, so we didn't spend a lot of time on that point either.

The third issue he raised was also somewhat familiar. He said, "Bill, according to the Bible, there is no antidote for sin. There is no way in the universe to overcome sin according to the Bible, except through the Son of God, Jesus Christ. You can't get over the sin problem by obeying the Ten Commandments, although everyone should seek to obey the Ten Commandments. Nor by belonging to a good church, because even though everyone should belong to a good church, the Bible doesn't teach that you can overcome sin by attending a good church. Nor can we do it by performing good deeds or tithing, though everyone should do good deeds and tithe. According to the Bible, the only known antidote for sin is Jesus Christ." I had heard something like that before.

However, the fourth point hit me like a ton of bricks. He said, "Bill, this antidote is not automatic. You don't become a Christian because you're an American, or because you live in the suburbs, or because you're a member of a church, or because your family members are Christians. Becoming a Christian is a choice. Would you like to accept Jesus Christ as your Savior right now?"

At that point, I understood little of what he was talking about, even though I did consider myself to be a Christian and had been going to church regularly. I really didn't understand the importance of his question. But by the grace of God, I did know the right answer and said, "Yes." He said, "Fine, let's pray." We bowed our heads and said a little prayer. As I did so, without fully understanding what was transpiring, I became a Christian in the biblical sense of the word—that is, a person in whom Christ lives. I didn't know it at the time, but subsequently I found out that in that instant, several things happened automatically. First, my sins had been forgiven. Second, I became a child of God. Third, I gained the assurance of eternal life in heaven with God the Father and Jesus, His Son. And fourth, for this life I received not a promise of no more troubles, but the opportunity to appropriate peace, joy, gentleness, self-control, and much more into my life.

On that afternoon I didn't know all of that. I knew something had happened, but I wasn't sure what. I didn't understand until much later some of the significant details. The first thing that happened was I had to go home and tell Ellen about this. That was a little awkward. It's not easy to go home and say to your wife, "By the way, today I had a life-changing experience in a public dining room with a man I never met before."

But we got past that. As a matter of fact, around the same time, Ellen made a recommitment of her life to Christ. And we began to try living with one another as a Christian couple and raising our children as a Christian family, only we didn't know much about how to do that. Our kids were doing fine. They weren't dropping out of school or using illegal substances or getting in trouble. But we realized we weren't providing them with the kind of spiritual leadership the Bible says Christian parents are supposed to give. So we began to try to do that.

"Just Like the Waltons"

The first thing that occurred to me was if we were to be a Christian family, we ought to all gather around the breakfast table and have a little Bible study every day. Much to the amusement of my children, that's exactly what we began to do. We developed this format: We began to meet at 6:45 in the morning, starting with a little prayer. Then we would read something from the Old Testament (frequently from Psalms) and then we would pray again. Next we would read something from the New Testament. Then we would break up and I would go to work and the kids would go off to school.

When we first began this family morning devotional, it was kind of a strange sensation. Somewhere I had gotten the notion, too, if you were a Christian family and you were going to pray together as a family, you all should hold hands around the breakfast table. So I proposed this. My son Wil was in kindergarten at the time. (He now is a graduate of a fine college, married with two children of his own, and the vice president of a financial institution.) As we gathered around the table—my daughter Anne, Wil, Ellen, and me—with our heads bowed and holding hands, Wil peeked up and said, "Gee, Dad, just like the Waltons." Except it was more like the blind leading the blind. The reality is, we didn't have a clue about what we were doing.

Here is an interesting thing we discovered: God evidently doesn't care about expertise. He didn't seem to mind that we didn't know the buzzwords, that we hardly knew one end of the Bible from the other. We just knew we were in the presence of the living God and we were going to pray together. Since then we have done this thousands of times. A lot of days it wasn't that much fun. Sometimes there was resistance from the children. Sometimes our hearts were hard. A lot of times there was tension, and other times we were too busy. But we just did it anyway, day after day, year after year.

Our children are grown up and have families of their own, so when we gather to pray in the morning, it's just Ellen and me and the dog. But I'll tell you, we have discovered the veracity of that old saying: "The family that prays together, stays together." It has bound us together in a way that cannot be described, other than just to tell you it has happened.

My new relationship with Christ also affected my relationship with my constituents. I went back and wanted to talk to them about Jesus. I'm sure I was not as tactful as I should have been. In fact, I scared some of them. One of my best political friends said, "Bill, we expected you to go to Washington and get Potomac fever. We didn't expect you to turn into some kind of religious fanatic." One of the newspapers even wrote an editorial that said, "If Mr. Armstrong is now so interested in religious matters, perhaps it would be a good idea if he did not run for reelection."

The truth of the matter is, I wasn't interested in religion per se; I was interested in a vital, personal relationship with Jesus Christ. As it happened, I *did* run for reelection and was reelected. Then I was reelected again. Then I ran for and won a U.S. Senate seat and was also reelected to that office. Before long, the novelty of somebody in Congress sharing his faith in Jesus Christ dissipated. What remained was the realization that someone whose life is accountable to Jesus

Christ is held to a higher standard than someone who just holds to a standard of obeying the law or a code of ethics.

A Life of Purpose and Meaning

So this is what has happened to me over these last two or three decades. But I want to be sure that as you think about what has transpired in my life, you don't conclude, "That's great. Wonderful. You have a unique story—one in a million." Because it's not one in a million.

What has happened to me is basically what happens to any person who asks Christ into his life. The Bible says, regardless of who you are, when you look to Jesus for salvation, your sins are forgiven. You become a child of God and have the assurance of going to heaven to spend eternity with God the Father and Jesus, His Son. For the remainder of your life on earth you can experience peace, joy, gentleness, and self-control—the ability to live a life filled with purpose and meaning.

One day, a wealthy man came to visit me in Washington D.C. His name can be seen routinely on the Forbes 400, meaning he is among the 400 richest people in the world—and he's not number 398, either. He's way up toward the top of the list, a man who really has everything from the world's perspective.

We went to lunch in the Senate dining room. I didn't know him very well, but I presumed he came to talk about pending legislation. We spent about five minutes talking business but then, to my utter surprise, he admitted he wasn't satisfied with his life, that he was thinking of selling his business, closing up his house, and moving his family to another city and starting over. In spite of all he had and all of his great achievements, he was miserable.

My response was to tell him, "God loves you and has a wonderful plan for your life. Because of sin, you cannot have the relationship with God that you would like to have.

And the only way to overcome sin is through the Son of God, Jesus Christ." Since we were in the Senate dining room, I didn't have the boldness to ask the fateful question, but a few days later, I was with him in his office and I did ask him. I said, "Would you like to accept Jesus Christ as your Savior?" And he said, "Yes." So we prayed together, and what happened to him is the same as what happened to me: he received forgiveness of his sins. He became a child of God on the way to heaven. He gained peace, joy, gentleness, and self-control he had never known before. In short, his life changed, and he became a Christian in the biblical sense.

Maybe not everyone can be a political leader or a business leader, but this showed me that everyone has the ability to be a spiritual leader and can lead other people to Christ.

The Crankiest Presentation of the Good News

A similar experience happened with one of the staff assistants who works on the floor of the Senate on Capitol Hill. In many cases, staff assistants are talented, highly educated, energetic, ambitious young men and women who work for senators or congressmen. Often they are the intellectual superiors of the people for whom they work and actually do a lot of the real decision-making. I thought of this young man as a crown prince of Capitol Hill because, although you wouldn't recognize his name, at a crucial moment in the life of this country he wrote a lot of very important legislation. He was a mover and shaker, although anonymous in doing so.

I had known this young man for years, but on one special day he came to my attention in a different manner than ever before. I was on the Senate floor, standing behind my little desk with a gigantic notebook under each arm. I had just offered what I considered a wonderful amendment to a bill. However, my Senate colleagues had the temerity to turn down my amendment. I was furious, just filled with anger.

I was standing there with my two notebooks under my arm, preparing to go back to the Hart Senate Building, where I could retreat in the privacy of my office to reflect on the great injustice I had just suffered, along with the downfall of Western civilization and whatever else I could think of to salve my wounded pride. Just as I was preparing to leave, my gaze fell on the young man I mentioned, this crown prince of Capitol Hill. I didn't hear an audible voice, but it was as if God spoke to me and said, "Today is the day I want you to talk to this young man about Jesus." I thought to myself, *Lord, not now.* But the impulse was irresistible.

So with books under my arm, I stalked over to this young fellow and I said, "Follow me." We went out the east doors of the Senate, down a short hall, and through another set of double doors, out onto the east steps of the Capitol Building. There was a gale-force wind blowing across the steps, and the young man had a dazed look on his face, wondering why I had summoned him. Still clutching my books and speaking through clenched teeth, I gave what I believe was probably the crankiest presentation of the good news of Jesus Christ ever heard in North America. I said to him, "God loves you and has a wonderful plan for your life." Then I told him about how to receive forgiveness for sin and salvation through Jesus. Finally, I told him, "Let's pray," and we said a little prayer together. With that I announced, "I have to go back to the office."

I didn't find out until a year later what happened. Even though I was the most unwilling of messengers, in that instant the young man also made a life-changing decision. His sins were forgiven and he became a child of God, assured of entry into heaven for an eternity, and much more that the Lord offers through His love and grace. I relate this story because it makes an important point: You don't have to be in a holy place to make a life-changing decision.

There is another example that's worth noting. Have you ever known someone who, when he or she came into the room, the room seemed to brighten up? This experience involved such a person. You just loved to see her coming because she was so cheerful and vivacious, with a big smile. She had a wonderful personality, lots of friends, and a good job. One day she came into my office and asked if she could close the door. She shared with me about her past—she had done something so terrible that she didn't think God could possibly forgive her.

Then she asked me a penetrating question. "I have heard you have a personal relationship with God. Could you tell me how I could also have such a relationship?"

I responded, "God loves you and has a wonderful plan for your life. But none of us, neither you nor me nor anyone else, can have the kind of relationship we would like to have with God because of sin. The only provision for sin in the entire universe is Jesus Christ, the Son of God. Would you like to accept Jesus as your Savior?" She nodded, then bowed her head, and in just a few moments, her life became changed for eternity.

Leadership, in my opinion, means living a life that others can see through. Christian leadership means living a life where other people can see Christ through you. She saw that I was a Christian. But she also saw that I was approachable about that most important dimension. Being ready to explain the hope we have is part of being a Christian leader.

Becoming Involved

Something else that I learned about being a Christian, though, may surprise some people. I am more convinced than ever that one of the responsibilities we have as Christians and often neglect is to become involved in the political process.

It was the Lord Himself who issued the definitive word on this subject. In Luke 20 is the familiar story where the Pharisees launched one of their periodic efforts to embarrass Jesus. They were always doing that. They thought it was clever to ask these questions, as if somehow they were going to put Jesus on the spot in a way that would be impossible for Him to evade. So they asked Him this very difficult question: "Teacher, we know that you speak and teach what is right, and that you do not show partiality but teach the way of God in accordance with the truth. Is it right for us to pay taxes to Caesar or not?" (Luke 20:21,22).

It was a very difficult question because if Jesus said, "Yes, it is lawful," that would outrage the Jews because the Jews didn't like to pay taxes any more than we do. But if He said the opposite, He would anger the Romans, and in that society it was not astute to get the Romans upset with you.

Verses 23-25 say, "He saw through their duplicity and said to them, 'Show me a denarius. Whose portrait and inscription are on it?' 'Caesar's,' they replied. He said to them, 'Then give to Caesar what is Caesar's, and to God what is God's.'"

Most people, when they think about that passage, realize that it draws a line in the sand beyond which government may not properly go—that government may not encroach upon matters of faith. You can't impose the government on the church.

But I think there is another conclusion that can be drawn from this passage. In this encounter with the Pharisees, Jesus Christ conferred upon the process of civil government—that is, the political process—a status and dignity that it never had before. In other words, when He said, "Give to Caesar what is Caesar's," He wasn't just talking about taxes. I believe He was talking about the duties of citizenship as well.

One of the Noblest Callings

In the first chapter of the first book of the Bible, human beings were given an obligation to take charge of the world. Dominion was given to them. And throughout Scripture we're instructed to be good stewards of the earth. I don't read anyplace where God gives us dominion over agriculture, fields, mines, businesses, and highways, but says, "By the way, the political process is out of bounds."

I don't want to be presumptuous here, but I think that our Lord was saying, "Take charge of the process of government as well." By the way, this isn't an original idea with me. John Calvin and theologians through the ages have felt that the process of government—the political process—is one of the noblest callings of a believer.

Scripture teaches us that God is cognizant even when a sparrow falls. Scripture teaches that He has numbered the hairs of our head. If God cares about such things, can it possibly be that He is indifferent to issues that are settled through the political process? If God cares about the sparrows, does He not care about income taxes and estate taxes? Does He not care about the laws that regulate family life? Does He not care about abortions? Does He not care about homosexuality? I am absolutely convinced that He does. Therefore, I think that He expects us to care as well.

If you can accept this premise, I want to suggest some very specific things that Christians are called upon to do to enrich, take charge of, and provide input to the political process.

Every Vote Counts

First, we are all called upon to register and vote. I want to tell you something shocking. I am almost certain that, in any given room of businessmen and women, many of them are not registered to vote. That means there are a lot of people in places of great responsibility who are not able to take even that elementary step in governing our country. Across the United States, among Christians and especially among evangelicals, there are millions of people who do not register and vote.

Why? In a handful of cases I think that people have a sense that somehow they shouldn't vote. It's not a common attitude, and I don't think there's scriptural basis for their attitude.

There are others who think that voting doesn't make any difference. I want to tell you, having spent half a lifetime in politics, that it makes an enormous difference. Over and over again, a pattern that I have seen is that a handful of votes, sometimes only one vote, can make a dramatic difference in the outcome of things. We only have to look back to our presidential election between George W. Bush and Al Gore to see how important every person's vote is.

I believe that registering and voting in an informed way is absolutely the minimum that any believer is called to do.

Second, I think that believers should take as a personal responsibility—literally, a calling of faith—to help candidates of their choice in a personal way. There are a lot of mundane but necessary jobs in a political campaign. A person can address envelopes or answer phones at a headquarters. Someone can go door-to-door and pass out brochures. People can stand out on street corners and wave signs. Things like that make a big difference. They don't have a lot of status. They don't have prestige. But I'm convinced that they can change the outcome of elections and thereby the destiny of our country.

Third, I think people should feel it a calling of faith to support candidates financially. I'm embarrassed by how many businessmen and women, people of means, are reluctant to make large contributions to political candidates. I think that's something we're called to do. When the Lord said, "Give to Caesar," I think that in a modern context it means to support candidates whose views mirror your own.

Fourth, I think it's the duty of believers to write letters to the editors of their newspapers. I used to own a newspaper, and I'll reveal a trade secret. Newspapers are not reluctant to receive letters to the editor. They love to get them. Many newspapers publish a high percentage of all the letters they get, if the letters are reasonable. In fact, at our paper, we published a lot of letters which were by no definition reasonable or even sensible. We just published them because they came in. The letters page is one of the most highly read pages in the entire paper. It's a great way to communicate because, in an odd sort of way, newspaper readers take more seriously the letters to the editor than they do the columnists, editorial pages, or news accounts. Somehow, letters seem more genuine. So if people have strong feelings, particularly if they see something that is important in the long term, they should write letters to the editor.

I also think it's the duty of thoughtful citizens who want to participate in the process to call in to radio talk shows. I admit that frequently these programs descend to a level of political discourse that I don't find very elevating. Sometimes they're crude. Sometimes the commentaries are kind of stupid. But the reality is that these are the town meetings of the twenty-first century, and if we aren't part of it, we're missing a great opportunity to participate in the process.

Fifth, I want to encourage people to get in touch with and stay in touch with their congressmen, senators, assemblymen, state senators—not just at election time, but more important, between elections. While I was in office, the EEOC proposed a rule to correct what they deemed to be religious harassment in the workplace. They had an idea—an ill-founded one—that there was a widespread problem of people being harassed over their religious beliefs or lack of religious beliefs in the offices and factories and shops and other workplaces of America. So they proposed a rule that was so sweeping that the practical result would have been to prohibit almost any kind of religious expression in the work environment. It would have meant literally that you couldn't wear a cross on your lapel. You couldn't have a Bible on your desk. You wouldn't be able to have the Ten Commandments or a picture of Jesus on your wall. Congress intervened and prevented that from going into effect. But the important thing to know is how that happened. *It happened because tens of thousands of people on very short notice got in touch with their congressmen and senators and said, "Put a stop to this."*

That issue and many others of importance are going to be coming back. I urge believers to be in touch with their legislators by mail, phone, or whatever. Better yet, they should find a way to get to know their representatives personally. It's hard to do if the legislators are in Washington, but when they're home, there are times when they want to get to know their constituents, and that's usually just before an election. Voters can maintain that friendship after the election, which puts them in a position to have a high-leverage contact and to speak up on a basis of long-standing friendship rather than on just a letter in the mail.

Run for Office?

Finally, and I say this cautiously, I hope there are some Christian leaders who will feel called upon to run for public office. It's a great experience. It's not for everybody, but I think we need to see a lot more men and women from the churches of our country run for the school board and for county commissioner and city council and Congress and the Senate and even for president. I believe that we can bring a perspective and understanding of human nature, a compassion, and a wisdom that's very important in the political mix. My own experience showed me that people were drawn to Christ in me simply because they didn't see much evidence of Christ around them at work.

How does a person know if he has been called to this? The same way we know if we're called to anything. It's a matter of prayer. I think God often speaks to us silently from the inside. Sometimes it is through the counsel of Christian friends. Obviously, the place God speaks to us most often is when we're in the Word.

I hope people will be motivated to think about the things I've mentioned: to register to vote, to participate in the campaign as a volunteer worker, to contribute financially, to write letters to the editor, to get in touch with the talk shows, and maybe even to run for office.

But as people consider these things, there are some guidelines we all need to keep in mind. I believe that these guidelines would make the above suggestions more doable.

We need to remember to pray for our leaders. Not just the ones we agree with. We're not supposed to pray for just the candidates who we think are on the right side of the issue. We're supposed to pray for *all* of them.

Let's remember also that it's wrong to throw the mantel of Jesus Christ over every political cause that comes along. Some issues have valid arguments for each side. I happen to be a passionate believer in having a Constitutional amendment requiring a balanced budget. But it would be blasphemy for me to say that is a Christian issue. It isn't. It's a good program, but I don't think Jesus Christ endorsed it. I don't think Jesus is a Republican or a Democrat or a conservative or a liberal.

Even though I think it's the duty of Christians to be more involved, I think it's dead wrong for us to portray politics as such an exclusive club that you have to be a Christian to run for office, or that only a Christian can serve with dignity and responsibility and integrity. If God can make sons of Abraham out of stones, He can certainly make good legislators, or good county commissioners, or good governors or presidents out of people who aren't Christians, or who aren't our brand of Christian faith, or who have not come out of our religious tradition.

We ought to participate. We ought to be leaders. But it's not an exclusive club. We should never try to be a power bloc. I think there is a real danger if the church makes a pronouncement on public issues. The church should prepare its people to participate as individual citizens, rather than try to position itself as a participant in the process. The church should stand above the process and evaluate it, not compete with it. The church's unique role is preaching the gospel and preparing believers for their own ministry outside the church.

We should never get bogged down in the debate over whether this is or should be a Christian nation. If you look at the trends, there are a lot of things that should give us cause for concern, but the bottom line is that God rules in the affairs of men and nations. God is in charge. We are not called to take the ultimate responsibility.

Finally, no matter how enthusiastic we are about the political process, and I say this as one who has been involved in it for a long time, we should never let anyone think our ultimate faith is in political parties or platforms or legislation or Constitutional amendments.

There is a lot we can do. There is a lot of good we can do. I pray that God will show good men and women of this country how they can be participants in this very important aspect of our society. I believe it is part of our calling.

This is a great country. But it will die before our very eyes if we do not seek for the answers to its problems where the true Source of change can be found. Change doesn't originate in Washington D.C., or a state capitol, or a county seat. It happens in hearts. It is our task as Christians and leaders to point the way to where true change occurs.

Twelve years ago, I attended a conference north of downtown San Diego at a lovely resort. The first day at lunch I sat at a table with nine other people, one of whom was Bill Williams.

Bill graduated from the University of Missouri in 1970 with a business degree, and briefly considered joining the staff of Campus Crusade for Christ. Instead, he felt that God wanted him to use his natural business skills and his degree, so he entered the medical profession by starting a company that made artificial hips and knees. The business was very successful, but in 1978 he sold the company and then joined the Navigators, an evangelical Christian organization, in their executive outreach area for five years.

He later returned to the business world as national vice president of marketing and sales for the Pyxis Corporation, a leader in the health industry. As the company grew, they did a very successful Initial Public Offering. Bill and his wife, Kathy, started the Faranhyll Foundation, whose purpose is to foster value-based leadership in corporate life, and funded it with Pyxis stock. A short time later, Pyxis sold to Cardinal Health for one billion dollars.

Bill and Kathy retired to a mountain property they bought in Colorado, and Bill resumed his relationship with the Navigators. Shortly thereafter he was asked by Cardinal to return to Pyxis as president and CEO, an offer Bill accepted.

Today, Bill and Kathy Williams are back in Colorado in their mountain home, where they oversee the Faranhyll Foundation. They are the parents of two adult sons.

17

The Loneliness of Command

Bill Williams

WHEN I THINK OF WHO HAS INFLUENCED ME most as a Christian and as a businessman, two people stand out in my mind. One is the late Art DeMoss, a successful business leader who was also committed to sharing Christ with everyone within his sphere of influence. Art DeMoss successfully bridged his corporate career with a life of ministry, and as a result, many businesspeople came to Christ through his influence. In so doing, he served as a model for my own life, because I share that same vision for ministry.

The other influence is Eric Liddell, the Olympic runner featured in the movie *Chariots of Fire*. Liddell's life resonated with me because he wanted to excel in his area of strength so that God would be glorified. He said that when he ran, he "felt God's pleasure." But he also had high standards, which he wouldn't compromise for the sake of his running. By taking a strong stand for Christ, he was a testimony to both believers and nonbelievers. That's how I've wanted to live my life.

Chariots of Fire came out when I was working full-time with a Christian ministry. God used that movie to challenge me to move back into the business world. I felt that God was telling me it was time to practice what I had been preaching.

My conflict with whether to stay in full-time ministry or move into business came at a very early point in my life.

Campus Crusade for Christ invited me to join their staff when I was in college because they felt I had evangelism gifts. But I really wanted to be in business. I felt very guilty about not being a vocational Christian worker. I didn't realize at the time that you could be in ministry and business at the same time!

A Spiritual Calling in a Secular Setting

My business interest was in the area of health care, and so that's where I began my career. Within a short time, I started and sold some companies in the surgical implant field. Then, still not sure of where I should be working, I joined the staff of the Navigators ministry full-time. Back then, I was one of the many Christians who had a segregated faith, believing that the Christian world was over to one side of my life and the business world was on another. There was no bridge connecting the two. But when *Chariots of Fire* came out, I realized that my time with Navigators had been a training period, preparing me to return to the business world so that I could be a vital Christian in a business environment.

Eric Liddell knew that he was called to a spiritual calling in a secular setting. I felt the same way about my life. He understood his gifts. And I think it's very interesting that today he's still better known for his running and the stand he took than for his missionary work in China. After I saw the movie I began to pray and seek God's direction in Scripture for where He wanted me. My wife and I asked God what our gifts were, and how we could best use them for God's glory.

As it worked out, not long after this I was on an airplane, seated next to a man who was on the board of directors for a medical company in California. We got to talking about each other's lives, and eventually he told me that my experience was exactly what they needed in his company. Would I consider consulting with them? I met with the president of the company, and our hearts were immediately drawn together. He then suggested that he would mentor me in his business if I would mentor him in his personal life. So I was hired initially as vice president of sales and marketing for the Pyxis company, and it eventually became one of the most successful publicly traded companies in the country. Stock went from three cents to 76 dollars, and eventually we sold the company to Cardinal Health for one billion dollars. In the meantime, my friend's life changed dramatically, and he came to understand his purpose in life as a child of God.

Those were exciting days. They were also stressful, discouraging, and sometimes overwhelming, but always with a sense of God's blessing. I know this because of how He kept using the *Chariots of Fire* theme song at different points along the way. On a plane coming back from a meeting where it looked like we were going to run out of money before we achieved our corporate goal, the song came over the plane's loudspeaker. In a hotel while I was on a very difficult trip where I worked long hours, got little sleep, and had no privacy, the piano player in the lobby played it. In the car, when I was feeling very discouraged about a meeting with the president, it came on the radio. During some of my most tiring, discouraging days, I repeatedly had this experience where I felt that God kept telling me that I was in His hands and things would be all right. I keep a detailed journal, and over a period of 16 years, well past the time when the song was popular, I have more than 30 citations of where that song broke through the low time and reminded me that I was being used by God to glorify Him. A particular situation still strikes me as one of the most remarkable experiences I have ever had.

A Leader with No Followers

After Pyxis was sold to Cardinal, I retired. All my worldly dreams had been realized. We were financially secure, which means I should have been happy, right? But as I sat at our family ranch, an emptiness crept in on me. I began to feel very distant from God. I felt that I was supposed to wait to see where God would lead next, but I became filled with anxiety. I was a leader with no followers, and it made me feel very empty.

Pyxis began experiencing some problems of its own after the acquisition. There was some downsizing, some unrest, and some corporate culture issues that were creating trouble, so the company called me back and asked if I would travel around to their regional areas to talk with the employees. One of the meetings was in Chicago, and we decided that, for a little recreation, we would go to Wrigley Field for a Cubs' baseball game. It was a beautiful April day, and we were eating hot dogs and peanuts, the Cubs were winning, and I was feeling good. I was in this classic stadium, surrounded by Pyxis people, thoroughly enjoying myself.

Then, between innings, when the grounds crew came out to groom the infield, the stadium intercom blared the theme song from *Chariots of Fire.* I hadn't heard it in a long time, and there it was, seeming like a message aimed directly at me. It literally jolted me. My mind became flooded with all the times the Lord's sovereignty and grace had sent that song to encourage me and point me to the model of how He wanted me to live. I didn't say anything to the guys around me, but in my heart at that very moment, I knew that I was going to be named the new president of Pyxis.

I had been president of a lot of things before this, but they were minuscule compared to a billion-dollar company. This was a humbling, frightening thought because it was lifting me right out of my comfort zone and back to the edge of my faith. I lost track of the baseball game and was full of excitement and fear simultaneously.

Sure enough, when I got back to my hotel that night, the chairman of Cardinal Health called. He said he was trying to figure Pyxis out and knew that I understood the culture, and asked if I would come by his office in Columbus, Ohio, to meet with him. "I need to pick your brain about Pyxis and what its needs are," he said. He penciled in 30 minutes on his calendar for later that week. It was pretty intense from the start, and it became a two-and-one-half-hour session. He asked me to come back and run the company, which I was happy to do. After the experience at Wrigley, I was expecting it.

Coming back as president is when I learned a lot about what God wants in a leader. I became convinced that God wanted to use Pyxis to create Christlikeness and maturity, and to bring people to Himself. What I learned about spiritual growth as it relates to business is in Philippians 2:5-11:

> Your attitude should be the same as that of Christ Jesus: Who, being in very nature God, did not consider equality with God something to be grasped, but made himself nothing, taking the very nature of a servant, being made in human likeness. And being found in appearance as a man, he humbled himself and became obedient to death—even death on a cross! Therefore God exalted him to the highest place and gave him the name that is above every name, that at the name of Jesus every knee should bow, in heaven and on earth and under the earth, and every tongue confess that Jesus Christ is Lord, to the glory of God the Father.

It says we should have the attitude that Christ had. Jesus didn't step into this life as a Pharisee, but as a carpenter. He stepped into the real working life. This helped me as I thought about segregated faith, of whether I could be an effective Christian even if I didn't work for some ministry organization. Some people say that if they're going to live as Christians, then they need to go to a Bible college or become a missionary. That's not necessarily true. At Pyxis I was walking into life in the same kind of reality as Jesus did. We face real situations, real dilemmas, real relationships every day, and God creates something in us through our experiences, then uses us to sculpt something similar in other people.

What does Paul say about Jesus? That He emptied Himself. He poured Himself out. How does that apply to us? When you carry the pressure and burdens as a CEO of a major company, it involves a lot of pain. But I look at Jesus, who made Himself vulnerable and approachable, and I see One who carried the pain and anguish without trying to hide it or hide from it. In my early days as president I didn't live like this. I pulled back and protected myself, cutting off access from others because it was such an emotional drain on me. I found myself getting angry about attitudes and office politics. Everything that comes to a president is a problem, an issue, a struggle, and a decision. I felt that I was surrounded by immaturity, and I found that my tolerance for people was diminishing at a rapid pace.

So when Jesus faces the likes of us, what does He do? In the midst of immaturity, selfishness, and politics He opens Himself up. Amid the barbs and the wounds is a depth of love and character. As I meditated on these verses, it became clear to me that God was saying, "Bill, I want to use Pyxis to teach you how to love the way I love, because the goal is to eventually make you a man of love. The kingdom of God is a place of love, tolerance, acceptance, forbearance, and understanding." When I understood what God was saying, I knew it was going to be painful. Loving this way hurts a lot, and I don't like to be hurt. Jesus knew that He would face pain, but He loved anyway.

Our management team developed a set of qualities that we hoped defined the kind of company we wanted to be. To those who looked closely, they could see that they were the qualities of Christ Himself. We said we wanted Pyxis to be a company based on 1) integrity, where we are honest and fair in our business practices; 2) quality, where our products reflect excellence; 3) honor, where we treat customers and employees with dignity, courtesy, respect, humility, and gratitude; 4) unity, using teamwork and handling differences in a positive, appropriate, and forthright manner; and 5) leadership, where we vow to remain optimistic, receptive to change, and listening to customers.

Learning Selfless Love

God began using Pyxis to make me more approachable and loving, to try to make me listen to Him when I had difficult decisions to make. It was His way of taking me to a deeper place. This is different from where I had been living, because I'm a type A, control-oriented, aggressive guy. At Pyxis I thought I could create, control, and manipulate whatever the company needed. But as it grew into a three-billion-dollar company, it got so big that I couldn't control it. This became a very humbling experience. Some people had a lot of anger and resentment toward me. They assailed my character. They accused me of things. As a result, there were numerous lawsuits filed against me. I would take these issues to God and He would say, "Keep loving and serving them. That's what Jesus did." God taught me to take my hands away from trying to change people. It's His job to change hearts, not mine.

This experience taught me selfless love. I had an image that I wanted to be a rock wrapped in velvet. I wanted to be stable, solid, and dependable, but I also wanted to be loving, kind, gracious, tenderhearted, and approachable—just like our Lord.

The real test came when I had to fire some people from the company. Some of them were Christians. One was a man I helped lead to Christ and had been involved in his spiritual growth. But in business you have to perform, and the numbers weren't there for this person. As the leader, I knew that I had to do this with love. So before he even came to hear the bad news from me, I made sure he had a positive severance package and outplacement service to help transition him to another job.

As I look at Jesus, I notice that He was real, transparent, vulnerable, and didn't protect Himself. He stepped into other people's worlds. That's what I tried to do. I looked at who I was becoming and who I was influencing. And I wanted it to be as close as possible to how Jesus lived.

This sense of embracing another's situation, of stepping into someone else's world, of being vulnerable, of being approachable, has one more element, and that is loneliness. The result of living the way Jesus lived was that they put Him on a cross and killed Him. That sounds to me like not everybody liked Him or understood what He was about. Most of us like it when people like us. We don't like it when others dislike us.

The Loneliness of Command

I was in an art gallery in New York, and I saw a beautiful etching of Robert E. Lee sitting in front of his tent with a forlorn look on his face. The work was titled "The Loneliness of Command." I knew when I saw it that it was what I was going to learn, so I bought it. It showed that there is a weight and a burden that goes with leadership. Lee lived in such a way that people respected him. A lot of leaders have to live with not being understood. That's how I felt when we were going through difficult times at Pyxis and many people lost their jobs. I was attacked not only for cutting back positions, but also for being a Christian. It was very painful and very humbling.

There is one more point that I get out of the verses in the second chapter of Philippians. Jesus fulfilled His ministry. He didn't just enter the real world, live out selfless love, and empty Himself to the point of being crucified. He also fulfilled the ministry His father sent Him to do. One of the things my wife, Kathy, and I started at Pyxis was a personal foundation so that we could hold chapel services after national meetings for whoever wanted to attend. It wasn't a company function—it was organized by my wife and me as a separate activity.

Not everyone was in favor of this, of course, and I got some pretty angry e-mails and memos. I even got a letter from the vice president for human resources, who is also an attorney, telling me that I had better not do this anymore. But my thought was, How does a company in the United States have the right to tell a private foundation when and where it will host a meeting? We weren't using Pyxis stationery or their resources. It was strictly word of mouth. God put a hedge of protection around it and used it to bring people to Himself. People found Christ through the foundation. It was a bright, shining time where the company took on eternal consequences in the lives of its employees. It created a spiritual connection for a lot of us, where we could pray for and support one another.

Correcting at a Deeper Level

When the company was going through a very difficult time, I felt that I could connect with other believers in the company at a level beyond just being business associates. I shared with them what God was teaching to me through Hebrews 11:27. The writer, speaking of Moses, said, "By faith he left Egypt, not fearing the king's anger; he persevered because he saw him who is invisible." Moses persevered through 40 years of waiting upon God in the wilderness, prior to the fulfillment of the call on his life. I doubt that those years were filled with peace and joy. I suspect they were filled with questions and frustration. I shared with the other people some observations about Moses that I believe God gave to me:

1. It is a natural tendency to want to claim a promise or fulfill a destiny in the power of our fleshly abilities.

2. God's timing is never our timing. It's always longer.

3. God will always deal with the character of His servant before fulfilling the promise.

4. We always think we are far more capable or ready to accomplish His work than we are.

5. Spirituality must be learned, and there are no shortcuts to maturity. The process is frustrating and often makes no sense.

6. We must be content with the small things He has placed in our way while we wait. Moses led sheep for 40 years before he led a nation. If we're convinced we're where God wants us to be, and we are bent on being faithful to Him, then small things do matter.

7. Enduring is not fun. But the resulting character of endurance is a mighty tool in the hand of God.

8. Times of endurance build our faith, trust, and reliance on God. They teach us the spiritual way to make a promise become a reality.

I wrote to the believers on our staff, "I think the present struggles that we have passed through and those to come are simply opportunities for us to experience a reliance upon His power. Let us resolve ourselves to that so we might experience His peace. If you look at the leadership of

Moses, you will see a habit of his taking every detail before the Lord, no matter how small. That should be our goal. Perhaps it is the fundamental lesson enduring is designed to teach."

Jesus showed us how it is done. He entered into our world and lived out His Father's call on His life. He made Himself vulnerable and approachable. He dealt with rejection. And He finished His ministry. That's what I want to do. I know it's not always fun, but it is deeply satisfying and there is an inner peace amid the strain, and a knowledge that He's taking me to a new place every day.

My challenge to other leaders is for them to think about their jobs, their aspirations in light of this. Do they see how God is using their leadership to do something in their hearts? Are they entering into the struggles of other people and paying the price with them, or are they pulling back and protecting themselves? Do they have the vision that Jesus had of being in the real world and seeing how it is affecting people? Are they willing to carry the rejection of leadership and the pain that comes with it, and let the Lord turn the bitterness of their hearts into real, deep, lasting love? That's what Eric Liddell did. It's what Art DeMoss did. It's what Moses did. It's what Jesus did. It's what I want to do.

Denny Shaw has a fascinating background, going back to Washington D.C. where he served as the undersecretary of the Defense Department and the Navy Department as well. His wife, Mistie, had been in the Army, finally retiring as a major after 22 years. After leaving public service Denny accepted a position with Pacific Ship Repair in San Diego, where he was a tremendous CEO, accomplishing a major corporate turnaround. Ultimately it was Denny's integrity and transparency that influenced his decision to walk away from his $200,000-a-year job.

Denny and Mistie live in San Diego with their three children. Denny is an adjunct professor at Point Loma Nazarene University.

18

Character Is More Important Than Success

Dennis Shaw

IT WAS A LATE MARCH 1989 AFTERNOON WHEN I drove slowly out of the VIP parking lot located directly in front of the Mall Entrance of the Pentagon. Taking a long and final look at the massive, five-sided, sand-colored building, I felt mixed emotions. I wanted to leave and yet I didn't.

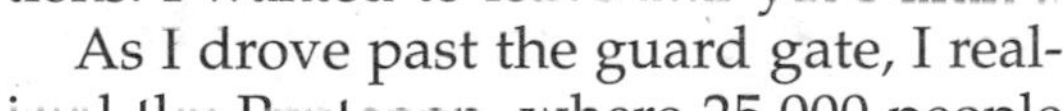

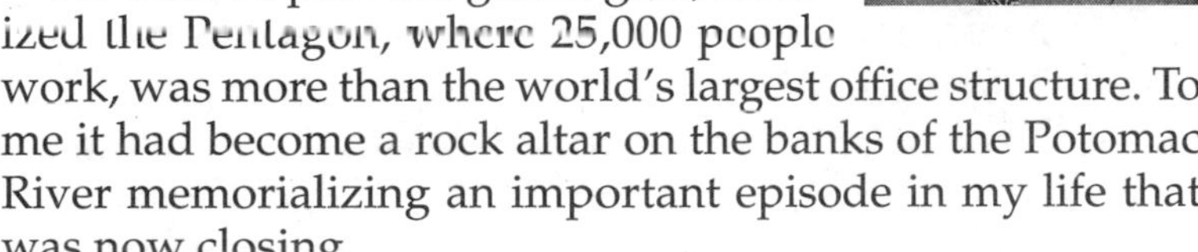

As I drove past the guard gate, I realized the Pentagon, where 25,000 people work, was more than the world's largest office structure. To me it had become a rock altar on the banks of the Potomac River memorializing an important episode in my life that was now closing.

That drive out of the parking lot ended more than seven incredible years of service as a political appointee in the Reagan Administration. From early 1982 until 1989, I had been the principal deputy assistant secretary of defense and acting assistant secretary of defense (reserve affairs) for Secretary of Defense Caspar Weinberger, the deputy under secretary of the Navy (policy) for Secretary of the Navy James H. Webb, Jr., and the special assistant for the National Defense Strategic Stockpile for Secretary of Defense Frank Carlucci. I began these political "tours of duty" at age 34 and was leaving as a senior citizen, I thought, at age 42.

Those jobs may sound rather dry to some people, but to me they were all awesome, and I had poured my life into doing my job well. But in so doing, there had been a price to pay.

From the day I arrived at the Pentagon until the day I departed, I worked harder and longer hours than I had ever worked, or perhaps will work, during my life. The demands upon me were severe and, at times, even brutal. As a result, I loved it and I hated it. But during the good and the bad, I had done a good job. With me, among the suitcases of clothes and office memorabilia in the trunk of my car, I carried the Department of Defense Medal for Distinguished Public Service (Gold) awarded by Secretary Weinberger and the Department of Defense Medal for Outstanding Public Service (Silver) awarded by Secretary Carlucci. The hard work, accomplishments, job titles, and medals were, as the world measures things, emblems of success. Unfortunately, as I said, this kind of success comes at a price.

My wife, Mistie, and our three children, Casey, Tim, and Jaimie, became wounded veterans of families with missing (never home) public servant spouses and parents. For seven years, Mistie single-handedly reared (fed, clothed, disciplined, nursed, educated, transported, cultured, and loved) our children while managing every facet of our household, including the finances. While I hadn't completely abandoned them, Mistie acknowledged my cameo appearances at home by occasionally introducing me at the dinner table. She also relentlessly admonished me to exhibit an appropriate sense of humility when taking out the trash. Her admonitions were purposely aimed at counteracting the surrealistic and heady effects of my pampered, privileged Pentagon life with its chauffeured sedans, military aides-de-camp, helicopter commutes from the Pentagon to awaiting military executive jet aircraft at Andrews Air Force Base, and the like.

Then in early 1988, following the resignation of my boss, Navy Secretary James Webb, Mistie decided enough was enough. "We," she declared, "are going home to California."

Mistie had earned and now asserted the right to make up both our minds. The timing of her decision coincided nicely with a huge family reunion she helped plan. After the reunion we went house-hunting in San Diego, where, prior to joining the Reagan Administration, we had lived and I had practiced law.

After finding a suitable house, we flew back to Washington D.C. Mistie quickly arranged the packing and shipping of our household furnishings, and she and our three children moved to our new home while I stayed on to complete my work at the Pentagon and wrap up the details of disposing of our house in Alexandria, Virginia.

A New Career

When I arrived in San Diego, I met with a friend who was the president and CEO of a company that repaired aircraft carriers and other Navy ships. He offered me a job as vice-president of government relations and marketing, no doubt because I was a friend and because I had been the deputy under secretary of the Navy. I remember saying to him: "I'm a lawyer. What do I know about repairing ships?" As I recall, he reminded me he was a lawyer too, didn't know much about repairing ships when he bought the company, and was doing just fine. What could I say? He did appear to be doing well, so I accepted his offer.

I have to be completely honest, though. I wasn't walking obediently with the Lord at that time in my life. The truth is that the salary he offered was attractive, and I needed to support my family. Also, I expected to have a lot of fun with my friend. It sounded like a good option, so I accepted the job without even bothering to pray about it—and that turned out to be a big mistake.

One day shortly after I started my new job, precisely at noon, the company was raided by the FBI, the IRS, and the NIS (Naval Investigative Service). Government agents swarmed all over the shipyard and wrapped it with plastic yellow tape like a Christmas package. They roamed outside and inside the shipyard wearing their dark blue jackets emblazoned with huge white FBI or IRS or NIS letters on the back. They confined us to the conference room in the executive office for about 12 hours while they boxed up and seized company records. They disabled all company phone lines. We couldn't contact our families, nor could they contact us, until about 7 P.M. that evening. Outside the shipyard, having been tipped off in advance, local television camera crews and reporters recorded and reported the raid.

I couldn't believe this was happening. The transition from my world at the Pentagon to this scene was bizarre, incredible, perplexing, embarrassing, and frustrating. While waiting and withering in the conference room, the words of William Bendix, who starred in the 1950s television show "The Life of Riley," came to mind: "What a revoltin' development this is!" I asked the invading government agents what the raid was all about. None of them would tell me. They were there to ask questions, not answer them, they said. The day following the raid, my friend—the CEO of the company—told me he believed the trouble concerned the former owners of the company.

The Calm Before the Storm

During the weeks and months immediately following the raid, various criminal and civil lawyers were retained, and we held lots of closed-door meetings. But after a while, things settled down and we carried on the usual business of repairing ships without the distraction of legal hassles with the United States government. From time to time, the U.S. Attorney's Office requested additional corporate documents, but I was reassured the raid only involved former owners.

Sometime during the late summer months of 1990, however, I began to get indications that all was not well; big trouble was brewing. Finally, in mid-October, I was made privy to what had been developing. A criminal indictment charging former owners and current officers and employees of the corporation, including the CEO, was imminent. Furthermore, a deal had been cut with the U.S. attorney. The company would not be charged with criminal felonies in the forthcoming indictment if the current CEO and certain officers and directors resigned. This deal was crucial, because a company charged with felonies is temporarily suspended from contracting (doing business) with any part of the federal government. If the company subsequently is convicted of the charges, it's then debarred from doing any business with the federal government for a certain period of time. The legal distinction between suspension and debarment is slight, but the practical distinction is nonexistent. Both operate as a death sentence for a company whose only business is repairing U.S. Navy ships.

The other shoe dropped on November 1, 1990. The U.S. attorney filed a 32-count indictment against former owners of the company, some current officers and employees, and my friend, the CEO. What was happening to my success? During my first year at the company I had attracted almost one million dollars in new ship repair work. Mistie and I were remodeling our home. I was earning good money. Everything had been going well. But now, what I thought were baseless allegations were turning into indictments, felony counts, resignations, plea bargains, deals with the Department of Justice, suspension, debarment and shutdown of the shipyard.

My first inclination was to run and get as far away from the company and its problems as I possibly could. But if I ran and the shipyard closed, what would become of the 300 to 400 hardworking blue-collar workers and their families?

I believed that by staying I could save the shipyard from closure.

I also believed my friend—now the *former* CEO—when he assured me he wasn't guilty. He claimed the indictment was the product of political hard feelings over his role in a recent mayoral campaign. I wanted to believe him, and I did believe him. I think I was in shock at the time, which dulled my senses and clouded my perceptions about somebody I really liked, who had helped me and whom I now wanted to help.

Another Emblem of Success?

My friend and other officers and directors of the company resigned on November 6, 1990, and I was elected president and CEO. Ordinarily, such a promotion would have been another emblem of success that I could have added to those I earned at the Pentagon. But not this promotion. I became the CEO because I was the only corporate officer left—the only tree standing in a forest ravaged by a firestorm. All the criminal activities alleged in the indictment had occurred prior to my joining the company in March 1989. I was not implicated. Now it was my turn to hire lawyers, as well as work with those already defending the company, and lead the fight to save the company from closure. My experience and reputation while serving as the deputy under secretary of the Navy, no doubt, would be useful.

In an attempt to demonstrate corporate responsibility, I immediately suspended with pay any mid-level employee who had been indicted, or named but not indicted. To my great surprise, this infuriated the assistant U.S. attorney. Unbeknownst to me, the deal that had been cut included termination, not suspension, of these employees—or so the assistant U.S. attorney said to me in a scathing letter that promised felony charges would be filed against the company if I didn't take action as agreed. I knew such felony charges would trigger suspension from performing government contracts. This would have put the company out of business, so I regrouped and terminated those employees I had just suspended.

This was extremely painful to me for several reasons. First, I knew that many of these people had been led down the primrose path. They didn't know, nor were they told, that the $1000 and $2000 political contributions that they had donated and which were reimbursed by the company were crimes. They were shipyard workers, not savvy, wealthy political partisans. The boss asked for the money, they gave it, and they got it back. What's the problem? Second, I had to do the dirty work, face-to-face, sacrificing the lambs by executing provisions of an agreement that I knew nothing about and that had been arranged by others. Third, I was forced to renege on my word that indicted employees would be suspended with pay pending the resolution of the charges in the indictment. It made me look callous and cruel. Had I known the terms of the deal that had been cut, I never would have suspended and then terminated these mid-level employees.

I also was faced with the prospect of debarment, and ultimate closure, from another source. The Department of the Navy, in addition to the Department of Justice and other departments and agencies of the federal government, can suspend and debar a company whose owners, directors, officers, or key employees have been indicted for criminal felonies. Since our company hadn't made a deal with the U.S. Navy as it had with the U.S. attorney, it remained exposed and vulnerable to potential closure if the Navy decided to suspend the company. When the Navy's Office of Procurement Integrity learned of the November 1, 1990, indictment, if it hadn't already learned about it from NIS raiders, we would be in for big trouble. Time was short.

The Need to Act Quickly

In situations like this, when integrity-type felony indictments have been filed against the owners, directors, officers, or key employees of a company, the company can, and most likely will, be suspended from doing any business with the federal government while the government decides what action it will take. Because the wheels of government grind slowly and exceedingly fine, a company dependent on government contracts could be out of business before the government decides what to do.

I had to act quickly. I didn't want to wait until the government decided what to do. I went to the government, told them what mistakes had been made, and ate humble pie in big bites. Then I told them what corrective actions we had taken to keep these mistakes from happening again. I assured them that the government was not at risk by continuing to do business with my company. Then I tried to negotiate a settlement.

I knew this was risky because it would displease government agents who might have preferred to suspend the company while negotiating a settlement agreement because it gave them more leverage. But the way I looked at it, the livelihoods of innocent employees were at stake. I had to risk offending someone while working my way through the long, arduous, and humiliating settlement process. The government agents would get over their pique, I figured.

I put my character and reputation on the line when I negotiated a settlement with the U.S. Navy's Office of Procurement Integrity. I had to do that if I wanted to save the company. And I *did* want to save it.

I signed an administrative settlement agreement in which I promised the Navy, among many other things, that I (including any other officer or director of the company) wouldn't permit the former CEO to directly or indirectly influence the business or operations of the company. I told

Navy representatives, to whom I was no stranger, I could prevent such influence and would prevent it. They accepted my assurances. They trusted me. But if I didn't honor my settlement agreement promise, the agreement would be breached and the Navy would debar the company. And my reputation would be trashed.

Why did the Navy demand that I promise not to permit the former CEO to directly or indirectly influence the business or operations of our ship repair company? After all, he had resigned. He was history. How could, and why would, he attempt to influence the operations of the company after having left? The short answer is that he owned 100 percent of the company's stock. As the sole shareholder and owner, he could control the company, despite having resigned as president and CEO, by electing compliant, obedient board of directors who appointed compliant, obedient officers. The Navy would have a problem with that.

The federal government doesn't do business with companies controlled by people indicted for, or convicted of, felony crimes. Without a doubt, the former CEO's stock ownership would be a paramount concern of the Navy in settlement negotiations. So when he resigned, the former CEO also put his stock in a blind trust and appointed a newly retired U.S. Navy rear admiral, rather than me, as trustee. This accomplished two things. First, since blind trusts were not yet banned by the government as a settlement remedy, the trust stopped the government from raising any "control" or "influence" objections during suspension and debarment settlement negotiations. Second, it kept me in check. I was the only remaining officer and director at the company; I had total control of its operations. This posed too much of a risk, or threat, to the sole owner of the company's stock. I might run the business into the ground. Or perhaps worse, I might run off with the business to enrich myself.

The United States Navy trusted me. I told the Navy the blind trust would work. I promised to make it work. With that assurance, the Navy didn't require the former CEO to sell his stock. And, boy, do I regret it. The following four years, from November 1990 to August 1994, were a nightmare.

Financial Stress

While negotiating a settlement agreement with the Navy, I asked the company's chief financial officer for a full report on the financial status of the business. To my shock—a feeling to which I was becoming accustomed—the company owed about $8 million in 30- to 90-day (short term) accounts payable. Accounts receivable met payroll and most of the expenses. The hard assets of the company were worth $1 million to $1.5 million at best. The company was in the hole nearly $7 million.

As the new CEO, I realized I was going to have to operate what looked like an ongoing Ponzi scheme—using current contract income to pay down old contract debt and future contract income to pay current debt. I got in my car, visited every vendor and subcontractor, and promised to cut every nonessential company expenditure and use every dime of profit to retire debt.

Once again I put my character and integrity on the line when I negotiated the forbearance of creditors. I had to do that if I wanted to save the company from the jaws of bankruptcy.

I brought in new people, put highly competent people in key positions, cut and cut and cut costs, sold every unnecessary piece of property, squeezed vendor and supplier bids to rock bottom, aggressively bid new ship repair contracts, and did a lot of tap dancing in the sand. There were ups and downs in our progress, and eventually we were able to increase our profit, decrease our debt, raise our workers' pay, and improve our facilities. We were even able to open a second ship repair facility in Seattle and increase the number of major new contracts we negotiated.

About 18 months after his appointment as trustee of the blind trust, the retired Navy admiral resigned citing health reasons and an upcoming move to the East coast. That was true. But it wasn't the whole truth. He didn't disclose that his health was threatened by disturbing telephone calls and bursts of anger from the former CEO. The admiral had reached the point where he no longer could tolerate the previous CEO's barrage of advice, guidance, direction, and criticism, which, implicitly, he was supposed to heed and use to govern me and the way I was running the company.

The Navy refused to approve the first individual nominated to become the successor trustee because relationship between the nominee and the former CEO appeared to be too tight. It took awhile, but the Navy finally did approve a successor trustee nominated by the former CEO. The new trustee elected himself to the board of directors and attempted to become familiar with the business of the company.

The former CEO eventually pled guilty to a few felony counts in the indictment, was sentenced by a federal District Court, and was debarred by the Navy for a period of five years. A never-ending series of problems associated with him kept distracting us from the regular business of the company. But we kept working hard, and the company continued to improve. I was earning more than $200,000 annually and life was good—not easy or stress free—but good.

A Turning Point

In the summer of 1994, on Mistie's recommendation, I enrolled in a Bible study called "Experiencing God," by Henry Blackaby and Claude King. There were 12 units in the program workbook, each containing five days of assignments. I completed the workbook reading and writing assignments every day during my lunch hour or at night at home. I memorized the assigned Scripture verse each week and attended a workshop every Wednesday night where students watched a video and then, in small groups, prayed and discussed that week's materials.

God used this program to teach and speak to me. His timing couldn't have been more perfect. In units one through seven, I learned about 1) knowing and doing the will of God; 2) being a servant of God; 3) walking with God; 4) pursuing a real, personal, practical relationship with God; 5) knowing where God is at work; 6) understanding how God speaks in different ways; and 7) exercising faith by choosing God's way, not my way.

Then I came to unit eight, "Adjusting Your Life to God." I didn't know it at the time, but unit eight in the "Experiencing God" workbook was God's means of preparing me for a spiritual test and real life crisis—a turning point where I had to decide what I believed about God. How I responded would determine whether I would go on to be involved with God or whether I would continue to go my own way. What I did revealed what I believed about God.

In June 1994, the successor trustee, who controlled the stock of the company and now was chairman of the board of directors, came to my office, closed the door, and directed me to hire back one of the former officers and directors who had resigned due to his participation in illegal campaign contributions, begin paying the former CEO payments that would amount to hundreds of thousands of dollars annually, and pay the legal fees of the former CEO. Furthermore, he told me that I was not to tell the Navy anything about this—that his directions were not to go beyond the walls of my office.

The chairman-trustee could not articulate one legitimate business reason for doing any of these things. We were just going to do them. It was clear to me he was communicating with the former CEO and taking direction from him, contrary to the terms and conditions of the Navy's approval of his appointment as trustee, and contrary to the promises I made to the Navy and the terms of the settlement agreement I signed.

If I followed the chairman-trustee's directions, the company would be influenced and controlled by the former CEO. That was a breach of the administrative settlement agreement, which would subject the company to debarment. If I didn't follow the directions, the trustee owner and chairman said he would fire me. This was a crisis. Putting my character and integrity on the line this time had a big price tag—giving up a $200,000-a-year job. Doing the right thing would be a major adjustment for me and my family, if not a disaster. This was a critical test.

Many questions crossed my mind. Could I do these things and cover them up? Should I? Would anybody ever find out if I did? What was the price of my character and integrity? Was the price too high? How important was it to honor the promises I made to the Navy? Do businessmen just walk away from high-paying jobs over character and integrity issues? Doesn't everybody have to make compromises from time to time? Shouldn't I simply find a way to rationalize things and then get on with it?

Be Willing to Walk Away

I remembered what Jim Webb, former secretary of the Navy and one of the smartest men I know, had told me several years before: "Never take a job you can't walk away from in a day." In other words, if I was so beholden to a job that I couldn't walk away from it, I probably would do anything to keep it, including sacrificing important principles and compromising character and integrity. That's not a job; it's captivity.

I also remembered the Scripture verse I had memorized recently in unit eight of "Experiencing God": "Any of you who does not give up everything he has cannot be my disciple" (Luke 14:33). Unit eight also contained several other lessons: 1) "If you want to be a disciple—a follower—of Jesus, you have no choice. You will have to make major adjustments in your life to follow God"; 2) "You cannot stay where you are and go with God"; and 3) "Obedience is costly to you and those around you. You cannot know and do the will of God without paying the price of adjustment and obedience."

There was no doubt in my mind that God was preparing me for another very important lesson. I needed to learn that God is more interested in my character than He is in my success. It was now time for me to decide which interested me more. Would it be God's way or man's way?

I submitted my resignation in August 1994 and advised the Navy I could not prevent the company from being influenced or controlled by the former CEO. I chose character over success. It was a difficult decision with painful consequences. But in making the decision and living through the consequences, I also learned what it means to be totally dependent upon God and free from fear.

I make less money now and I don't appear to be as successful as I used to be. But I have something now I never had before, the assurance that I'm truly walking in the Light, where Christ in me is visible in secret and in public. That has made it worthwhile.

When my wife and I moved from Denver to San Diego, I worked with the McColl family to expand the ministries of the Fellowship of Christian Athletes (FCA). We made plans for a fund-raising banquet so we could afford a full-time director, and it seemed natural for us to honor Bill McColl, a local orthopedic surgeon, and his wife, Barbara, as FCA couple of the year.

Bill is a former All-American football player at Stanford, and an eight-year pro tight end with the Chicago Bears, and has been a significant supporter of FCA. Bill's oldest son, Duncan, was an All-American defensive end at Stanford in 1977, and the FCA National Athlete of the Year. His son John is on the San Diego FCA board.

In honoring the McColls, Mike Ditka, who followed Bill as the Bears' tight end, came in from Chicago to be the keynote speaker. Donn Moomaw, a national FCA trustee, was our master of ceremonies. As we showed a movie of Bill's athletic accomplishments and his and Barbara's contributions to the community as humanitarians, it was abundantly clear that we had chosen the correct couple. We raised enough money to hire a full-time area director.

Bill worked his way through medical school playing football for the Chicago Bears, and graduated with a specialty in orthopedic surgery. Upon graduating, he and Barbara took their family of six small children, ages 1-6, to Korea where Bill served for two years as a medical missionary. His area of interest, in spite of his degree in orthopedic surgery, was leprosy. He not only worked with leprosy in Korea for two years, but also went on to be the chairman of the board of the American Leprosy Missions.

Several years later I asked Bill to give his life story to a group of local businessmen, and he was willing to be so transparent that he proved you can be an All-American, a Hall of Famer, a nationally renowned orthopedic surgeon, a father of three boys and three girls, and it's still all right—in fact, it's extremely important—to be transparent.

19

Living with an Eye on Eternity

Dr. William McColl

SEVERAL MONTHS AGO I WAS TALKING TO A longtime friend and spiritual adviser. This man had been a pastor for 40 years and had weathered many personal storms. These included an infant grandson with a malignant tumor on his liver, a wife who died from cancer, and the ongoing tragedy of an adult son disintegrating into schizophrenia. When I mentioned that my life of more than 60 years had been spared from tragedy, he said, "Just wait. Your time will come."

He was right.

Not long ago, our 15-month-old grandson drowned in our swimming pool. Despite heroic efforts by paramedics and the staff of Children's Hospital, Evan Angus McColl failed to regain consciousness. After watching him on life support for four days, we finally let him go.

This was a life-changing experience. But as a Christian I can put his death in a context that has me looking differently at my time in this world.

I date the onset of the journey of my soul to December 1958, when I went to a church family camp in Michigan. I had a three-year-old son, twin daughters who were one-and-a-half, and a six-month-old son. At this camp I met a pastor who laid on me the responsibility of a Christian father. Soren Kirkegaard said, "The trouble with Christianity or the idea of trying to become a Christian is that it suffers the fate of all radical cures. One puts it off as long as possible." I chose not to put it off any longer. I returned from that camp, began teaching Sunday school, and became part of a men's covenant group.

Personally, I never had a dramatic conversion experience, nor have I rebelled against the church. My story is rather bland compared to some. I was born in San Diego and grew up during the Depression. My family said a blessing at mealtime, a prayer at bedtime, and we went to church on Sunday and watched my dad sit in the back row and sleep through the sermons. But that Christianity rubbed off on us. My brother and sister and I all married Christians, retained an active church involvement, and remained married to our original spouses. Among us, we have 13 children, and 12 are active in the church.

I went to college at Stanford, entered medical school after my junior year, and played my last year of college football as a medical student. In 1951, Stanford had a good year, and we went to the Rose Bowl. I made the All-America teams, and was subsequently drafted by the Chicago Bears. I transferred to the University of Chicago Medical School, returned to Stanford for my internship, took an orthopedic residency in Chicago, and played eight years with the Bears. During this time I married my Stanford sweetheart, and we had six children in rapid succession.

Missionaries to Korea

In 1962, Barbara and I and our six children, ages one to six, went to Korea as missionaries with the Presbyterian Church. I worked with leprosy patients and orphans and helped train Korean doctors. During that time, Barbara sent out a newsletter to our family and friends. Here is an excerpt from what she wrote in 1963:

Just before Thanksgiving I went with Bill on one of his rounds to an orphanage, one that he has taken a special interest in because many of the crippled children had been sent here. The children were sitting on the floor, huddled together with their hands and feet under a blanket trying to keep warm.

Bill had a few children walk from one side of the room to the other, looking for limps, hunchbacks, unusable limbs. The others would laugh as several struggled to walk. Their clothes were rather shabby and they had no night clothes to change into at the end of the day.

The feeling I have inside of me is indescribable as I return to my home of six well-fed, well-dressed children, and I'm sure you, too, would feel the need to help in some way to make life a little more enjoyable for these children. Bill feels the Korean lady in charge has a real interest in the children and is doing the best she can with the small resources available.

Once a month or so on weekends, the U.S. Army would fly me up to the military camps in the demilitarized zone between North and South Korea. I would stay with the chaplain, give a football talk to the troops on Saturday evening, and preach the sermon on Sunday morning. This proved to be one of the better contributions I made as a Christian in Korea, serving as a pastor to the chaplains. In this experience I saw that believers need each other.

Like all Christians, priests, missionaries, and chaplains need Christian fellowship. Father Damien, who lived with the leprosy patients on the island of Molokai in Hawaii, used to beg his bishop to send him a priest for just a day to hear his confession and to pray with him. Dietrich Bonhoeffer, the pastor who led an underground seminary during the days of Nazi Germany, wrote,

> God has willed that we should seek and find his living word in the witness of a brother, in the mouth of man. Therefore, the Christian needs another Christian who speaks God's word to him. He needs him again and again when he becomes uncertain and discouraged. He needs his fellow man as a bearer and proclaimer of the divine word of salvation. The Christ in his own heart is weaker than the Christ in the word of his brother. His own heart is uncertain. His brother's word is sure.

This is why it is important to meet in small groups to share each other's burden.

When we returned to America in 1964, I was zealous for the Lord. But our marriage was having problems. My wife felt I was overbearing in my Christianity. I felt that she was undercommitted. We went to counseling, and I was fortunate to get a Christian man every bit my match. I respected his insights. Although he approved of my desire to be the patriarch of the family, he pointed out the fine line between the patriarch and the tyrant. Christian zealots sometimes cross that line. I know that I did. It was a lesson I have never forgotten.

My spiritual heroine became Mother Teresa. She was both a mystic and a missionary. The world knows her missionary heart. These words of hers reveal her spiritual insight:

> Jesus has chosen you. He has called you by name, and every day you have to say yes to be where God wants you to be. If He put you in the street, if everything is taken from you and suddenly you find yourself in the street with nothing, you must accept being in the street for that moment.
>
> This is the difference, to accept whatever He gives, and to give whatever He takes with a big smile. This is the surrender to God: to accept all the people that come, the work that you happen to do.

Acceptance of and surrender to the activity of God involves making a choice. I can illustrate this out of my own life. I heard a speaker who said that the major problem with 70 to 80 percent of Christian men is pornography. This surprised me, but then I've had my own bout with this evil habit.

Several years ago, if I was staying in a hotel alone, I would turn on an adult movie. This progressed to occasionally renting an adult video, viewing it at home alone, and copying it. I had three in my home library, and I would occasionally sneak a peek when I was sure the rest of the family was asleep. For some reason not clear to me, this activity stopped. My indulgences became limited to *Playboy* magazine during my visits to the barber.

Choosing to Surrender

Then one day I heard Jim Dobson talk on the evils of pornography and that it flourishes only because people buy it and look at it. I decided that I could make do with *Reader's Digest* at the barber, and I haven't looked at *Playboy* since. Mother Teresa says the purpose of life is to love God and to become holy. My choosing *Reader's Digest* over *Playboy* was a step on the road to holiness. One of the ways we love God is to surrender ourselves to God. That involves choice.

Chuck Colson wrote an article in *Christianity Today* about the massive crime bill that Congress was debating. They appropriated a lot of money to study the question, "What causes crime?" Colson said that they were asking the wrong question. Instead, he said, we should be asking, "What causes virtue?" All of the studies about crime find that crime is rooted in the way people think. Our thinking guides our choices. Choices become habits, and habits create character.

C. S. Lewis answered the complex question of crime, virtue, and holiness for us. In *Mere Christianity* he said,

> Every time you make a choice you are turning the central part of you, the part of you that chooses, into something a little different from what it was before. And taking your life as a whole, with all your innumerable choices, all your life long, you're slowly turning this central thing either into a heavenly creature or a hellish creature, either into a creature that is in harmony with God and with other creatures, and with itself, or else into one that is in a state of war and hatred with God, and with its fellow creatures, and with itself. To be one kind of creature is heaven—that is joy, peace, knowledge and power. To be the other kind means madness, horror, idiocy, rage, impotence and external loneliness. Each of us at each moment is progressing to the one state or the other.

When we're progressing towards the heavenly creature, we're becoming holy. For me, choosing *Reader's Digest* over *Playboy* was progress.

Now, back to the loss of my grandson. We live on the south end of La Jolla in San Diego, overlooking Pacific Beach, Crystal Pier, and Mission Beach. On Saturday morning the beach is full of joggers, some running in groups of three or four, maybe even ten. On one side of Crystal Pier is a jogger's plaque with the mileage to various landmarks along the way, such as the roller coaster or the jetty. The inscription on the plaque reads, "The Robert Martin Levine Sports Memorial, in memory of the many hours we ran together." I wonder about Robert Levine, and who it was who cared enough to hang that plaque.

A few weeks ago we were on a cruise ship from Miami to the Bahamas. The ship stopped at Nassau, which has a rich history of pirates and Spanish and English. I browsed in Christ Church Cathedral, the oldest English church in Nassau, first built in 1670, destroyed by the Spanish in 1684, rebuilt in 1695, destroyed again by the Spanish in 1703, rebuilt again in 1724, and then replaced with a stone building in 1753. On the walls of the sanctuary are plaques in memory of previous parishioners. One was for sailors lost at sea. Another was placed by crew members who lost 11 comrades to yellow fever.

One plaque read:

In memory of Emma Clementine Blatch
Died Nassau, October 16, 1825
Age 19
Reader, whoever thou art,
let the sight of this monument
imprint upon thy mind,
that young and old, without distinction,
leave this world.
Fail not to secure the next.

After some thought, I decided that this was the work of her grandfather. A husband or parent might have added "loving wife," or "beloved daughter." But grandparents, even though they may be grieving just as deeply, often convey a more spiritual message.

In the first half of our lives we focus on the present—our families, our jobs, who we are, how far we've come. We share a sense of immortality with youth. We attribute the high-risk activities of teenagers, such as drugs, random sex, joy rides, and guns to the fact that youth considers itself immortal. After 40, we see more clearly that life is finite. Normally, in peacetime, sons bury their fathers. In wartime, fathers bury their sons. But the truth remains, as it said on that plaque, "young and old, without distinction, leave this world."

"Remember Me"

Before he died, as I stayed by my grandson's bedside, and I prayed for him and with him, he and I began to communicate on a deeper plane. Evan worried about the effect his accident might have on his family; he knew they would miss him. How would this all shake out? He loved his grandma, and he loved her house; he loved to pull Rosy's tail and to hide under Grandma's desk, and to romp in the Jacuzzi with his mom and dad and his grandpa and B.J. and Meredith and Scott and Andrew. Would this all change? Would the joy they had at Grandma's house still be the same?

I told him I didn't know, but that we would place this in the hands of God, just as we would place him in the arms of Jesus. And I promised him I would make him a plaque, and this is what it would say: "Love God, live today, and remember me in the breaking of the bread."

The pastor friend I mentioned earlier told me that the only formula he knew for survival was to love God and to trust God even when loving and trusting God was hard.

Loving God is the first and greatest commandment. And so the first words on Evan's plaque are *Love God*. These are from me and the over-50 generation.

The next words on Evan's plaque are *Live Today*. They are from the generation of his parents, especially his Uncle Milt. With the help of his brother, Milt survived a crisis of his own. He is speaking from the heart when he says "live today." Sir William Osler once said, "The load of tomorrow, added to that of yesterday, carried today, makes the strongest falter."

Evan's plaque makes this last request: "Remember me in the breaking of the bread." This is for the generation under ten. The Sunday after Evan's accident, the grandkids went to church with Grandpa. The younger ones went to Sunday school, but B.J. chose the sanctuary with me. It was communion Sunday, and our minister opened the service with a beautiful prayer for Evan and the family. When it came to the sacrament itself, he pointed out that Jesus spent the last hours of His life with His friends. Evan spent his last hours with his friends: his grandma and grandpa, his mom and dad, his brothers and sister, frolicking and having the best time in the Jacuzzi.

When the pastor concluded with a commandment to "do this in remembrance of me," B.J. and I took our bread and juice together, and I thought, "Yes, Evan, this we will do in remembrance of you today—and evermore."

Evan is buried in the family plot where my parents and my grandparents are buried, and where I expect I will also be laid to rest. When that happens, Evan will have the company of his grandfather, his great-grandfather, and his great-great-grandfather. The common grave marker carries the message of Evan's plaque, along with some words from Peter Marshall: "Those we love are with the Lord, and Jesus has promised to be with us. If they are with Him, and He is with us, they cannot be far away."

Securing the Next World

When I remember Robert Levine's plaque on Crystal Pier, or Emma Blatch's plaque in Nassau, I think of Evan, and affirm that both young and old, without distinction, leave this world. Our time is short to secure the next. How do we secure the next? The apostle Paul says, "And now these three remain: faith, hope and love. But the greatest of these is love" (1 Corinthians 13:13). William Barclay says that faith and love depend on the hope that is laid up in heaven. The Christian hope is that God's way is the best way; that the only happiness, the only peace, the only joy, the only true and lasting reward is found in the way of God.

Loyalty to Christ may bring troubles here, but that's not the last word. The world may laugh at the folly of the way of love, but the foolishness of God is wiser than the wisdom of man. The Christian hope is the certainty that it is better to stake one's life on God than to believe the world. Or, in the classic words of Jim Elliott, "He is no fool who gives what he cannot keep, to gain what he cannot lose."

In tragedy, people like to quote Paul's words from Romans 8:28: "And we know that in all things God works for the good of those who love him." I don't know about that yet. In Evan's case, we will wait and see. I do know that Evan's and my worst fears did not materialize. Grandma's home is still enjoyed by Evan's parents and his brothers and sister just as before. The swimming pool and the Jacuzzi, where Evan drowned, is still a center of fun and activity for them, just as before, as it is for all his cousins. We now are expecting our fifteenth grandchild.

What has changed is the care and caution we exercise in trying to keep the little ones from falling through the cracks. We keep the pool covered whenever any at-risk child is in our home. This diligence is exercised by every cousin from the four-year-olds on up. Little Lauren, age four, told me the other day that we cover the pool because Evan had an accident.

For Duncan and Emily, Evan's parents, it meant a reevaluation of priorities. Six months after Evan's death, they moved back to New Jersey to enroll as full-time students in Princeton Theological Seminary. They are now completing their second year. Duncan will be a parish pastor, Emily a hospital chaplain.

For me, all of this was a stunning realization that young and old, without distinction, leave this world.

I have been faithful to my promise, and I remember Evan in the breaking of the bread. Now in my communion meditation, I also remember my parents and grandparents, other members of my family, and some special friends in Christ whom I might not otherwise have remembered. I have also written my own epitaph. What is good enough for Evan is good enough for me: "Love God, live today, and remember me in the breaking of the bread."

So remember, we need each other, we can sometimes be overbearing, our choices point us toward heaven or hell, and young or old, without distinction, leave this world. But Jesus has shown us the way to secure the next, and the words for Evan are our words, too: Love God, live today, and remember each other in the breaking of the bread.

The author may be contacted for speaking engagements at:

Dwight L. Johnson
Christian Catalysts
P.O. Box 6453
San Diego, CA 92166-0453

Phone or fax: (619) 222-3688
E-mail: dwight@cts.com

Dwight L. Johnson is a successful businessman and president of Christian Catalysts, a parachurch ministry. Among Dwight's many professional achievements was the design of the landmark Cross of the Rockies, the largest lighted cross in the world, located 15 miles southwest of Denver.

Dean Nelson is the founder and director of the journalism program at Point Loma Nazarene University in San Diego. He is a journalist who has written for the *New York Times*, the *Boston Globe*, *Christianity Today*, and several other national publications. This is his seventh book.

Other Harvest House Reading

Quiet Moments with God
by Lloyd John Ogilvie

Do you seek quiet moments with the Father? Do you long for His wisdom as you face daily decisions and challenges? Satisfy your heart's desire and open yourself in His presence, learning to humbly trust and follow His gracious leading.

A Father for All Seasons
by Bob Welch

A Father for All Seasons celebrates the wonder of the father/son relationship and shows how everything in life changes when the two connect. A joyful and candid look at the love between fathers and sons.

A Look at Life from a Deer Stand
by Steve Chapman

Taking you through his successful and not-so-successful hunts, Steve shares the skills for successful hunting—and living. With excitement and humor, he shares the parallels between hunting and walking with God.